This deeply pastoral book shows how suffering creates beauty in us just as long pressure turns ordinary material into diamonds. Christians are called neither to stoicism nor despair before adversity but to face it as Christ did, going through death to resurrection. A highly accessible Christian theology of suffering.

—**Tim Keller,** pastor emeritus, Redeemer Presbyterian Church

This is an extremely tender yet powerfully thoughtful volume that will help you embrace God through every affliction. For what Scott has written here is a definitive guide that will help every sufferer find their way back to hope, wholeness, and spiritual health. I give this remarkable book a double thumbs-up!

—**Joni Eareckson Tada,** Joni and Friends
International Disability Center

This wonderful, hope-infused book reminds us how God takes hard and ugly experiences and uses them to craft tenderhearted beautiful people. You shouldn't read this book just once; pull it out every couple of years to remind yourself that because of God's grace, hurt and fear don't win—beauty does.

—**Paul David Tripp,** author, *New Morning Mercies:*
A Daily Gospel Devotional and *Suffering: Gospel*
Hope When Life Doesn't Make Sense

Scott gently lifts our weary heads to behold our Father's grace and the glorious hope that we have in Christ to show us that our suffering is not in vain. This is a book that provides gospel-saturated meaning to our suffering, and it is a book that every Christian should read and read again.

—**Bryan Loritts,** teaching pastor, The Summit Church

T0051215

Scott Sauls gives us a most needed word of healing and regeneration at a time when so many of our words are utterly wounding. For those whose trauma and pain seems large or small: read this book and be prepared for God to draw forth your beauty, emerging as it will beyond your imagination and from the places you would least expect.

—Curt Thompson, MD, author, *The Soul of Desire* and *The Soul of Shame*

What Scott shares in this book provides meaningful help in addressing the depression, anxiety, and mental-health crises that have enveloped our culture. God makes beauty out of our regret, hurt, and fear. We are grateful for a seasoned, graceful, and humble guide like Scott Sauls to show us how.

—Sissy Goff, therapist and author of *Raising Worry-Free Girls*, and David Thomas, therapist and author of *Wild Things: The Art of Nurturing Boys*

I read everything I can find by Scott Sauls, and I can't help but think this might be his best book yet. Too many of us feel we have to hide behind an image of confidence and stability and put-togetherness. This honest, vulnerable, hopeful book shows us another way and does so with clarity, candor, and kindness. You will be glad you read it, and you'll want to read it again.

—Russell Moore, *Christianity Today*

Jesus' path to beauty and glory through suffering belongs to all his people in some measure. My brother and friend Scott Sauls has given us a gift. With pastoral sensitivity and care, he takes us to the heart of a beautiful God who wastes none of our tears.

—Irwyn L. Ince Jr., author, *The Beautiful Community: Unity, Diversity, and the Church at Its Best*

TEARS ON MY SHIRT

As we're coming out of a season of communal and personal loss, this book reads like a rope ladder of mercy, lifting us out of the pit of suffering and into the sunlight of God's wisdom. Scott makes space for our brokenness and gives testimony to the grace that delivers us out of the low places of our shame and sorrow, up onto the high ground of God's strength.

—**Sandra McCracken,** singer-songwriter and recording artist

Each time I turned a page in this book, I felt less and less alone. Scott understands my woundedness because he has been there. And as we walked together, chapter by chapter, he exposed the lies I've told myself, replacing them with the truths of God. This is a trustworthy guidebook toward healing and hope, written by a man who cares.

—**Al Andrews,** founder, Porter's Call

In Isaiah 61:3, God promises to turn ashes to beauty, mourning to joy, and a spirit of despair to praise. But how? In this life-giving book, Scott Sauls pulls back the curtain on God's redeeming love—a love that restores and heals beyond our wildest imaginations. Read it and take heart. Our God will restore all that is broken, even us.

—**Hannah Anderson,** author, *Turning Days:*
Lessons from Nature, Season, and Spirit

This is the book we need to understand that our weariness is not a burden to Jesus, the church, or our own growth as believers. Sauls invites us to embrace struggle as part of the human experience and to take heart in the fact that "when we are weak, he is strong."

—**Rachel Joy Welcher,** author, *Talking Back to Purity*
Culture; editor, Lexham Press and *Fathom* magazine

If you're in search of a book selling a gimmicky God who seeks fickle followers, leave this one on the shelf. But if you're open to a God who is far better than what we can conceive or control, and an author-pastor who has lived some harsh realities and dared to plot out a faithful way to sustain the Jesus journey, I urge you to read the wisdom in this book.

—A. J. Sherrill, author, *Being with God*;
lead pastor, Saint Peter's Church

You hold in your hands perhaps one of the greatest treasures for sinners and sufferers—like me, like all of us. Stories shared, hope offered, and biblical insights revealed in these pages speak directly to our crippling fears. Scott reminds us that our darkest stains and deepest wounds will never be wasted if we take small, faithful steps to entrust our "worsts" to Christ.

—Mattie Jackson Selecman, author, *Lemons on Friday: Trusting God through My Greatest Heartbreak*

Scott Sauls pens hallowed words. Though we are pelleted by adversity, loss, and pain, he helps us become more pliable to Christ and the Spirit that we may walk in cadence with our creator. This book overflows with wisdom, everyday tactics, and aha! moments to help you live the beautiful life you're meant for. Don't miss this stunning gift to all of us.

—Margaret Feinberg, author, *More Power to You*

Scott Sauls shows us how God's grace is at work in our sorrows and how God's ways are learned in the crucible of our afflictions. I found this book—equal parts personally vulnerable and pastorally wise—to be my favorite of Scott's books to date, and one I can't wait to share with others.

—David P. Cassidy, pastor, Spanish River Church; author, *Indispensable*

BEAUTIFUL PEOPLE DON'T JUST HAPPEN

ALSO BY SCOTT SAULS

*Jesus outside the Lines: A Way Forward for
Those Who Are Tired of Taking Sides*

*Befriend: Create Belonging in an Age of
Judgment, Isolation, and Fear*

*From Weakness to Strength: Eight Vulnerabilities
That Can Bring Out the Best in Your Leadership*

*Irresistible Faith: Becoming the Kind of
Christian the World Can't Resist*

*A Gentle Answer: Our "Secret Weapon"
in an Age of Us against Them*

BEAUTIFUL PEOPLE DON'T JUST HAPPEN

HOW GOD REDEEMS REGRET, HURT, AND FEAR IN THE MAKING OF BETTER HUMANS

SCOTT SAULS

ZONDERVAN BOOKS

ZONDERVAN BOOKS

Beautiful People Don't Just Happen
Copyright © 2022 by Scott Sauls

Requests for information should be addressed to:
Zondervan, 3900 Sparks Dr. SE, Grand Rapids, Michigan 49546

Zondervan titles may be purchased in bulk for educational, business, fundraising, or sales
promotional use. For information, please email SpecialMarkets@Zondervan.com.

ISBN 978-0-310-36346-0 (audio)

Library of Congress Cataloging-in-Publication Data

Names: Sauls, Scott, author.
Title: Beautiful people don't just happen : how God redeems regret, hurt, and fear in the
    making of better humans / Scott Sauls.
Description: Grand Rapids : Zondervan, 2022. | Includes bibliographical references. |
    Summary: "Regret, hurt, and fear are familiar to us all. Often we feel trapped in
    their grip, but it doesn't have to be that way. Scott Sauls is our empathetic guide to
    the freedom that is found in God—freedom that unburdens us from regret, hurt, and
    fear and opens the door to a new life of relief, contentment, and hope"—Provided by
    publisher.
Identifiers: LCCN 2022005008 (print) | LCCN 2022005009 (ebook) | ISBN
    9780310363446 (trade paperback) | ISBN 9780310363453 (ebook)
Subjects: LCSH: Suffering—Religious aspects—Christianity. | Pain—Religious
    aspects—Christianity. | Fear—Religious aspects—Christianity. | Regret—Religious
    aspects—Christianity.
Classification: LCC BV4909 .S287 2022 (print) | LCC BV4909 (ebook) | DDC
    248.8/6—dc23/eng/20220223
LC record available at https://lccn.loc.gov/2022005008
LC ebook record available at https://lccn.loc.gov/2022005009

Scripture quotations, unless otherwise indicated, are taken from the ESV® Bible (The Holy
Bible, English Standard Version®). Copyright © 2001 by Crossway, a publishing ministry of
Good News Publishers. Used by permission. All rights reserved. • Scripture quotations marked
KJV are taken from the King James Version. Public domain. • Scripture quotations marked NIV
are taken from The Holy Bible, New International Version®, NIV®. Copyright © 1973, 1978,
1984, 2011 by Biblica, Inc.® Used by permission of Zondervan. All rights reserved worldwide.
www.Zondervan.com. The "NIV" and "New International Version" are trademarks registered in
the United States Patent and Trademark Office by Biblica, Inc.®

The author is represented by Ambassador Literary Agency, Nashville, TN.

Cover design: Meg Schmidt
Cover illustrations: Meg Schmidt / Charunee Yodbun / Shutterstock
Author photo: Kylie Mathis
Interior design: Sara Colley

Printed in the United States of America

22 23 24 25 26 27 28   /LSC/   14 13 12 11 10 9 8 7 6 5 4 3 2 1

To all who sin, suffer, or feel afraid. The Lord is near, and your best days are still future.

To the wounded healers: pastors and ministry leaders, therapists and mental-health advocates, addiction counselors and sponsors, spiritual directors, healthcare and social workers, caregivers, embattled parents, and friends who keep showing up. I hope these pages will offer strength for you and those who are blessed to receive your care.

To the Spickard family. We live in hope.

CONTENTS

The most beautiful people we have known are those who have known defeat, known suffering, known struggle, known loss, and have found their way out of the depths. These persons have an appreciation, a sensitivity, and an understanding of life that fills them with compassion, gentleness, and a deep loving concern. Beautiful people do not just happen.

—Elisabeth Kübler-Ross,
Death: The Final Stage of Growth

ACKNOWLEDGMENTS

To Bear Rinehart, Andrew Peterson, Holly Williams, Kevin Twit, Dave Haywood, Nathan Tasker, Trent Dabbs, Tom Douglas, Keith and Kristyn Getty, Drew and Ellie Holcomb, Abner Ramirez and Amanda Sudano, Ben Rector, Sandra McCracken, Taylor Leonhardt, Jeremy Casella, Andy Gullahorn, Taylor Swift, Thomas Rhett, Bob Dylan, Jason Isbell, and Brandi Carlile. Thank you for writing redemptive songs, some of which kept me company in my efforts to write redemptive prose.

To Chip Dodd. You show me the path forward by taking me back. I am a better man for how you help me think, feel, and dream like a child. I'm still caught somewhere in the prologues. But the scent of Home is growing stronger, the songs are getting louder, and the ogre is getting quieter. This book could not have been written without your influence. You will recognize your fingerprints in certain places. And? I love you too.

To Wes Yoder, Webb Younce, and the Zondervan team. You're so good at this.

To Patti, Ellie, Abby, and Jeff. I thank God for giving me you.

To our Christ Presbyterian family. Thank you for singing hopeful songs loud.

To Tim and Kathy Keller. Thank you for showing that these pages can be lived.

To the boy and girl from high school and prologues 1 and 8. I'm sorry.

Y ou suck."

When someone said this to me recently, it wasn't the sound of the words that surprised me as much as it was the person who said them. The insult didn't come from a stranger on the internet, an upset church member, a partisan antagonist, or some other usual suspect. Instead, it came from someone I have known my entire life. This person understands me inside and out. I am closer to him than I am to anyone else, including my brother, my children, and even my wife. The person who told me that I suck was me. I said the words out loud while hiking alone. It slipped out of my mouth impulsively, as if from a primal instinct, without premeditation and straight from the heart.

Out of the heart the mouth speaks.

Lodged in my heart at the time was a shameful memory of meanspirited words I had spoken to another person in public. My words had been crafted to harm, targeting a fragile, vulnerable place in her soul. I wanted to injure and humiliate her. It was cruel, and I was cruel. I have replayed this incident in my mind many times. I offered several apologies and received her forgiveness each time. Eventually, she insisted that I stop apologizing because we were approaching the seventy-times-seven mark.

The hurtful incident for which she and God forgave me, and because of which I recently told myself, "You suck," happened thirty-seven years ago. It's been almost four decades but still feels like yesterday. Like a familiar song or movie, the memory has become part of me. Like the damned spot that Lady Macbeth tried frantically but unsuccessfully to erase.

I will say more about this story later in the book. But for now, I mention the incident to illustrate how second nature it is for us to hold on to things we've thought, said, or done that make us feel ashamed. Regret from the past dies hard for us. The one whom the Bible calls "the accuser" throws it in our faces, keeping memories about the worst things we've done so alive that in our minds, they start to define us.

"I said something mean" becomes "I am mean."

"I did something ugly" becomes "I am ugly."

"I made a big mistake" becomes "I am a big mistake."

Guilt (the regrettable things we have done) can so easily turn into toxic shame (the regrettable worms that we are) as we appraise our own worth. The interplay between guilt and toxic shame becomes, for some of us, a distinction without a difference.

Whenever toxic shame gains a foothold, things like grace, forgiveness, and new mercies leak out of us like water passing through a drain hole. It's almost as if we're hardwired for self-loathing, trapped in its grip like a tired, demoralized, wing-clipped eagle stuck in a birdcage.

One of the main reasons why I wrote *Beautiful People Don't Just Happen* is to help people stuck in the birdcage get their wings and freedom back. There is a bright blue sky of forgiveness and grace for demoralized, defeated souls. The air space is unlimited and free. Freedom is what God wants for us. Even as I write this, I pray that the ugly things from your past would lose their grip on you. I pray that you will come to understand that even though the ugly things are part of your story, they don't define you. I pray also that the eyes of your heart will be opened to receive the grace that is greater than the very worst thing about you. You couldn't escape it if you tried because as sure as his tomb is empty, the goodness and mercy of Christ will follow you all the days of your life.[1]

Regret is not the only thing that has had me trapped in the birdcage. If you have read my other writings or listened to my sermons, you may recall that I have experienced depression from time to time. I have had other hurts also. I have buried a few family members and lost some friends to suicide. I have been immobilized by hypochondria and chronic sickness, diminished by insomnia and fatigue, discouraged and made lonely by rejection, aggrieved by loss and death, humiliated by gossip and slander, demoralized by fear and failure, and traumatized by abuse from my childhood. Being a deeply flawed and sinful man, I have also brought some hurt on myself and others. I know the wearying effects of holding a grudge, living in denial, nursing toxic shame, and injuring people that I love.

Although I am familiar with pain, I have never contemplated self-harm. But there have been times when I told God that I had nothing left to give and would be fine if he took me Home. In hindsight, I'm very glad that he chose not to do this, because the darker and sadder seasons of life have served, ever so reliably and consistently, to expand my belief in and experience of the goodness of God. Through pain and sorrow, I have been tutored in the counterintuitive nature of his ways. I have learned that the greatest strength comes through the avenue of weakness, the

---

1. Ps. 23:6.

greatest wisdom through the avenue of disorientation, the greatest joy through the avenue of sorrow, and the greatest worship through the avenue of doubt.

As Melville said bluntly, "Heaven have mercy on us all—Presbyterians and Pagans alike—for we are all somehow dreadfully cracked about the head, and sadly need mending."[2]

And mend the cracks in us, Jesus does.

If these ideas feel foreign or bothersome to you, I hope they will start to feel more familiar and welcomed as you work your way through these pages. I believe that God wants to do this work in you as you seek from him a wisdom that is higher than your own, and a peace that transcends human understanding. Growing in the ways of God to become a more complete version of yourself is a lot like making a long-term commitment to physical fitness. The path toward becoming spiritually strong works a lot like good nutrition and exercise do.

When you first start working with a trainer at the gym, her command that you do twenty-five pushups before quitting can feel like too much. With each subsequent pushup on that first day, you feel like you are getting weaker. But the truth is—and the trainer knows this—you are getting stronger. If you keep coming back and submitting to the discomfort, you will soon be able to do twenty-five pushups with ease, then later fifty, seventy-five, one hundred.

The human soul under the disciplined regimen of God works like muscles do under the disciplined regimen of a trainer. The more the soul is worked and stretched to its limits, the more able it becomes to endure suffering and enjoy God all at once. When this happens in us, we become the best kind of dangerous.

---

2. Herman Melville, *Moby Dick* (New York: Scribner, 1902), 71.

The more we get pushed, the more pushing we can do, and the more able we become to show up for others in *their* toil and tribulation. When God's children start showing up for each other, the accuser starts to tremble.

God assigns purpose and meaning to the hurt we feel, even when we can't see his hand clearly. His approach is never punitive and always instructive, even surgical. As a self-proclaimed physician for the mending of body and soul, our Lord never stabs his children as with a sword. Instead, he only cuts us, ever so carefully, as with a scalpel. He wounds us sometimes, but always and only to heal us.

"In your struggle . . . endure hardship as discipline; God is treating you as his children . . . God disciplines us for our good, in order that we may share in his holiness. No discipline seems pleasant at the time, but painful. Later on, however, it produces a harvest of righteousness and peace for those who have been trained by it."[3]

The first time I heard these verses from Hebrews was when an older Christian man introduced me to them after someone broke my heart. I was upset with him for choosing these verses. I didn't want to hear that my pain had a mysterious purpose, much less that God was somehow behind it. Looking back, I realize now how shortsighted I was for being upset. I would later discover that these were the perfect and truest words for the season, and they have been for many seasons since. Sometimes we can't see the truth about God and ourselves until we see it in a rearview mirror.

Whatever hurt you may have faced or are facing now, I hope that *Beautiful People Don't Just Happen* will help you avoid wormholes like cynicism and despair, and instead discover—as

3. Heb. 12:4–11 NIV.

the apostle Paul did even from a hot, filthy prison cell—what he famously called "the secret of contentment." This secret, he tells us, is something that he had to learn, in the same way that Jesus learned obedience through the things that he suffered. Paul's secret did not come home to him naturally, but supernaturally. When it did, he found contentment and even joy in times of plenty *and* in times of want, in times of gain *and* in times of loss, in times of happiness *and* in times of hurt. "I can do all things," Paul wrote, "through [Christ] who strengthens me."[4]

I want you to know Christ as Paul did, and as I am learning to know him also. *Beautiful People Don't Just Happen* is written, in part, to assist you in this. As you read on, I pray that the secret of contentment in times of want, loss, and other things that hurt will become less of a secret and more of a familiar friend for you, just as it has become for me through the years.

Finally, I hope that this book will help you with any anxiety, worry, or fear you may carry concerning the future. The best advice I have ever received about my habit of "focused meditation on imagined, future worst-case scenarios" (aka, worry) came nearly thirty years ago from an older mentor in the faith named Jerram Barrs.

At the time, Jerram was an esteemed professor at Covenant Theological Seminary, where I was studying to prepare for pastoral ministry. It was an anxious season for me because of an undiagnosed illness that resembled other diseases that were terminal. I have since experienced healing from that illness, but at the time I was gripped with worry about where the mysterious

---

4. Phil. 4:10–13.

illness might be headed. "What if I die young?" I would say to Jerram in a panic. "What if I never get to have a wife or a family or a church to serve? What if?"

Jerram, who in those years became a sort of father figure to me, reached out and held me in a tight hug for several minutes. He also shed some tears, as he was known to do, in his characteristic empathy for anyone who experienced distress. After my shoulder was saturated in his tears, Jerram poured me a cup of tea and began gently challenging my imagined "what if" scenarios with things that are true.

"If you die young," he said, "then you will be with the Lord and all reasons for worry will be erased from your life. When we are afraid of what the future holds, we must not forget, Scott, that to live is Christ and to die is gain.

"If you die before marrying a wife or having children," he continued, "then you will have a story similar to both Jesus and the apostle Paul. Neither of these men were married or had biological children. Both died at what we call a premature age, just as most of the apostles did. And yet, as history has proven, they were still able to live full, meaningful, and fruitful lives.

"If you die without ever being called into ministry, you will instead become part of the great cloud of witnesses that the book of Hebrews tells us about. From that place, you will be able to cheer on and intercede for—directly and face to face with Christ—the work that continues through others, until he returns. You will also be spared many of the hardships that come hand in hand with faithful ministry."

For the record, it was the long embrace, the cup of tea, and the tears on the shoulder of my shirt, combined with the fact that Jerram had himself suffered greatly, that helped me hear his true words with a heart receptive to hope. True words are more easily received and metabolized when offered in a setting of empathy, understanding, and love.

The final thing Jerram said to me was, "Scott, in our moments of deepest worry and fear, when we catastrophize about the future, when we imagine the very worst for ourselves and for those we love—the thing we must do again and again is to talk to ourselves more than we listen to ourselves."

⌇⌇⌇

You'll notice that most sections in this book are referred to not as chapters but as prologues. This is my feeble attempt to remind us that we are, until we meet Christ face to face, a people in waiting. We are not Home yet. That's the hard news. The hopeful news is that Home awaits.

Because we are not Home yet, we need help developing a framework, a vocabulary, and stories to assist us in the work of talking to ourselves more than we listen to ourselves. The shaming voice of regret *can* be silenced with the countervoice of divine forgiveness and grace. The dehumanizing voice of hurt *can* be silenced with the countervoice of divine compassion and presence. And the immobilizing voice of fear *can* be silenced with the divine countervoice of a Savior who will never leave us, a love that will not let us go, and future promises that will never let us down.

I pray that *Beautiful People Don't Just Happen* will so familiarize you with the divine countervoice that the noisy shadow side of regret, hurt, and fear will fade into the distance. As the noise fades, I pray also that it will be silenced, rendering regret, hurt, and fear powerless over your heart.

PROLOGUE 2

A SCENTED CANDLE

The last year has been difficult. As I write this, the year 2020 has finally come to a close. It was quite a year, the best summary being a meme of five adjacent portable toilets, all of them on fire. The caption reads, "If 2020 Were a Scented Candle."

The cumulative trauma of a global pandemic, escalating unemployment, record rates of loneliness, depression, domestic abuse, and death, empty arenas and churches, doors shuttered on once bustling restaurants and places of business, rioting in the streets, discord in our homes, prejudice in our hearts, and the most troubling political campaign in modern history has taken a toll. For many, it feels like earth's foundations have been shaken.

My own foundations have also been shaken as I have, at this moment of writing, lost contact with 60 percent of the congregation I serve. People's retreat from church life is understandable, given the raging effect of a microscopic, fiercely contagious, and sometimes deadly virus called COVID-19. Nevertheless, losing touch with so many of our people because of the virus has made being a pastor even harder and lonelier than it has ever been otherwise.

Before this pandemic began, a well-known church-research expert released an essay called "How Many Hours Must a Pastor Work to Satisfy the Congregation?" Based on research in which those surveyed were asked how much time they expect their pastors to spend on prayer, sermon preparation, outreach, counseling, visitation, administrative functions, and so on, the total number of hours expected was 114 per week.[1]

Since the pandemic began, pastors' workload has increased with fewer volunteers and even more work to be done as everything also goes virtual. Twenty-twenty was an election year, which has added to everyone's stress. As the pandemic rages on, so does our raging. Petty politics replace more life-giving pursuits like faith, hope, and love. Many Christians have been drawn into the abyss of turning party platforms into their doctrine, pundits into their prophets, and politicians into their Jesus. Outrage is at an all-time high, and some people are at the end of their wits.

In such a climate, criticism toward pastors has increased, perhaps because people feel they have no other non-retaliating place to go with their stress. A few weeks ago, I received an anonymous letter in which a disgruntled member invited me to quit my job and find something to do elsewhere. The upset member signed off by saying that if I don't leave the church, then they most certainly will. Sheep can bite hard sometimes, especially the anonymous ones. People say that we pastors shouldn't read anonymous letters. But when you're in the isolation of a pandemic and lockdowns and "social distancing," sometimes you just can't help yourself, because even hurtful contact can feel more welcome than no contact at all.

The same church expert also wrote an article called "Six Reasons Your Pastor Is about to Quit." In addition to the reasons given in his earlier essay, others include personal weariness from the pandemic, financial stress, discouragement about losing

---

1. Thom S. Rainer, "How Many Hours Must a Pastor Work to Satisfy the Congregation?" *Christian Post*, July 26, 2013, www.christianpost.com/news/how-many-hours-must-a-pastor-work-to-satisfy-the-congregation.html.

members, members bickering with one another about how to respond to the virus, and above all, feelings of loneliness and abandonment. "Imagine your own mindset if one-half or more of your friends stopped engaging with you," the church expert said. "Pastors are burned out, beaten up, and downtrodden. Many are about to quit."[2]

That's how we pastors see our congregants. Not as our customers, pupils, ego boosters, donors, or anything of the sort. We view our congregants as our friends, our people, even our families. This year, most church life has gone virtual, which means I have spent more time staring into video cameras than I have into people's faces. While our people can see me as they worship and receive teaching at home, it is easy for them to forget that I cannot see them. I miss them. Loneliness accompanies one-way talking, one-way body language, and one-way expressions of love.

Personally, I have no interest in quitting my job like many other pastors apparently do. In my case, there are about fifty warm gestures sent in my direction for every ugly one. The anonymous letter writers are few and far between compared with the encouragers. I have also received hundreds of cards and thank-you letters from grateful members who are eager to return to our life in community together. Most of our people are the kind who speak words that make souls stronger. These are also the ones who sign their letters.

If you are a pastor (or an educator or administrator, a health-care worker, or are in food services or in some other essential work) who feels weary from serving on the frontlines, discouraged about this or that, and are perhaps receiving letters with words

---

2. Thom Rainer, "Six Reasons Your Pastor Is about to Quit," Church Answers, August 31, 2020, http://churchanswers.com/blog/six-reasons-your-pastor-is-about-to-quit/.

aimed at injuring you, I hope that these words from Theodore Roosevelt in 1910 will be as helpful to you as they have been to me: "It is not the critic who counts; not the man who points out how the strong man stumbles, or where the doer of deeds could have done them better. The credit belongs to the man who is actually in the arena, whose face is marred by dust and sweat and blood; who strives valiantly, who errs, who comes short again and again, because there is no effort without error and shortcoming; but who does actually strive to do the deeds; who knows great enthusiasms, the great devotions; who spends himself in a worthy cause; who at the best knows in the end the triumph of high achievement, and who at the worst, if he fails, at least fails while daring greatly."[3]

I also lost my mother this year. After ten years of Alzheimer's-related decline, time ran out in what affected families call "the long goodbye." I didn't shed any tears when she died—not because I didn't love her but because a decade of incremental, ascending grief was already behind me. By the time Mom died, I was out of tears and prepared to release her into heaven's care. I can't think of anything positive to say about Alzheimer's. I won't even try. It is a cruel, demoralizing, life-sucking disease.

Recently, I enlisted the services of a counselor. In my sessions with him, some uncomfortable things about my life—and about *me*—have been uncovered. In the uncovering, the counselor recommended that I add a trauma specialist to my treatment. As

---

3. Theodore Roosevelt, "Citizenship in a Republic," speech delivered at the Sorbonne in Paris, France, on April 23, 1910.

it turns out, I am less whole than the optics on my life suggest. I have good health, a loving wife, two brilliant and beautiful daughters, a church that loves us, some excellent friends, and fulfilling work. But behind the curtain of this wonderful life of mine, there also exists a small, sometimes scared, self-doubting man whose story includes the forementioned hard realities. I am a mess, a busted-up sinner who is dreadfully cracked about the head and sadly needs mending. Every person you meet is fighting a hard, hidden battle.

The past year has felt like too much. Like a pile-on.

Sometimes I wonder, why all of this? Why all at once?

Do you ever feel this way?

I am an American who has been shaped to expect comfort. Because of this, I am vulnerable to cynicism, moroseness, and self-pity when my outside and inside worlds betray expectations. The cultural air I breathe has trained me to think that life should be more carefree, predictable, and in control than it is. Having been among the world's privileged minority for most of my life, luxuries like good health, decision-making power over what and how much I eat, higher education, physical safety, social networks, clean water, and access to things I need *and* want have felt more like entitlements than luxuries. I have never buried my own child or experienced irrecoverable theft. I have never suffered violence because of my faith, hunger, poverty, sustained unemployment, or a terrorist attack. I have never been trafficked or kidnapped. I have never spent a night out in the cold or in prison. I am a white, wealthy, American man. As such, I have been conditioned to expect that life—*my* life—will run smoothly.

I have also spent many years ignoring some betrayals and injuries from my past, which my counselor is helping me process at age fifty-three. It's never too late to ask for help. The combination of expecting ease on one hand and denying my own trauma on another has left me lagging in my ability to live fully in a fallen world. But there is hope for change. As an elder said as he led our church in prayer last Sunday, "Lord, this has been a year filled with disruption, isolation, confusion, illness, and death. We ask for relief, but not without the revival of our hearts."

There are heart-reviving lessons that preach loudest through pain. As C. S. Lewis said, "Pain insists upon being attended to. God whispers to us in our pleasures . . . but shouts to us in our pain. It is his megaphone to rouse a deaf world."[4] One such lesson is that the world, as it is, is not our final home. No matter how hard we try to make it so, this present world refuses to be our paradise. We cannot make heaven happen for ourselves because heaven can only be given and received. When we accept and receive this truth, the revival of our hearts is made more possible. Being awakened by God's pain-megaphone redirects our focus to essential things worth preserving and nurturing: relationship with family and friends, rhythms and practices leading to health, humble service toward our work, our churches, and our neighbors, and above all, anchoring our roots in the character, promises, and future of God.

Mercy reveals itself through weariness.

I am not alone in realizing this.

Many of the world's greatest souls became their best selves not in spite of but because of their distress. Cowper wrote hopeful hymns and Van Gogh brushed epic paintings while contemplating suicide. Spurgeon preached some of his best sermons while depressed. Lincoln, Churchill, and King battled

---

4. C. S. Lewis, *The Problem of Pain* (New York: HarperOne, 2009), Kindle.

melancholy. Beethoven went deaf. C. S. Lewis buried his wife after a short, cancer-ridden marriage. Frankl, Wiesel, and Ten Boom survived the Holocaust. Ann Voskamp lost her sister and Joni Tada her ability to walk in tragic accidents. Christine Caine suffered abuse and Tim Keller got incurable cancer. John Perkins endured jail, beatings, and death threats from white supremacists.

As grief expert Elisabeth Kübler-Ross famously noted, "The most beautiful people we have known are those who have known defeat, known suffering, known struggle, known loss, and have found their way out of the depths. These persons have an appreciation, a sensitivity, and an understanding of life that fills them with compassion, gentleness, and a deep loving concern. Beautiful people do not just happen."[5]

Beautiful people. The ones we admire. The ones who change the world for good. The ones we like and want to be like. These people do not "just happen."

This axiom, that beautiful people do not just happen, also demands our attention in Scripture. Job lost ten children, his wife's affection, his livelihood, and his reputation in a single day. Moses stuttered. Jacob limped. Sarah was infertile. Tamar and Bathsheba were assaulted. David was betrayed by his son. Hosea's wife fell into prostitution, as did Rahab. Ruth was widowed in her youth. Mordecai was belittled and bullied. Jeremiah battled depression, as did Elijah. Gideon doubted God, as did Thomas. Mary and Joseph sought asylum from a reign of terror. Mary and Martha buried their brother. John Mark was rejected by Paul. Peter hated himself.

And Jesus wept.

---

5. Elisabeth Kübler-Ross, *Death: The Final Stage of Growth* (New York: Scribner, 2009), Kindle.

As we read the Bible, it is important to see that so many of the books—both Old Testament and New—were authored by someone who was enslaved, seeking asylum, in prison, facing persecution, or under another form of distress.

Beautiful people do not just happen.

And?

Sometimes the deepest, truest faith feels more like defeat than it does victory.

CRASH HELMETS
IN CHURCH

Among the beautiful people whose best attributes were formed through trial was the prophet Isaiah. I am honored to introduce (or reintroduce) him to you.

In the sixth chapter of his famous prophecy, Isaiah writes about how the Lord appeared to him in the year that King Uzziah died.[1] The loss of Uzziah was no small thing. He had been an exceptional leader, presiding over decades of peace and abundance. But the year that King Uzziah died became a marker for Israel, a bleak turning point as national flourishing gave way to Assyrian oppression. The emerging superpower invaded this smaller nation of God's people, killing their soldiers, assaulting their women, enslaving their children, pillaging their property, and scorching their land. For years to come, the memory of King Uzziah's reign would trigger a feeling that Israel's best days were behind them.

In a matter of months, what had once been light became darkness. There was no further prospect of a rising sun. It felt worse than a pandemic.

Conditions after the year that King Uzziah died were torturous. And yet, as Isaiah's book unfolds, we find that his deepest distress came less from his outer world and more from the inside. Just as a counselor can uncover trauma that's been buried in the subconscious, a direct encounter with the Lord—whom Isaiah

---

1. Isa. 6:1.

called his "Wonderful Counselor"[2]—uncovered the true nature of the prophet's own heart.

Isaiah records an experience of seeing the Lord sitting on a throne, high and lifted up, with the train of his robe filling the temple. Above the Lord stood a host of angels—all of them morally perfect creatures—who covered their faces and shouted, "Holy, holy, holy is the LORD of hosts." The temple shook and was filled with smoke. In response, Isaiah cursed himself, saying, "Woe is me! For I am lost; for I am a man of unclean lips, and I dwell in the midst of a people of unclean lips; for my eyes have seen the King, the LORD of hosts!"[3]

First the death of a beloved leader, then a terrorizing military invasion, then the stripping of a nation's history, identity, and way of life. We might say the year that King Uzziah died was Isaiah's version of 2020 or worse. But the weighty stuff of earth felt light to him when compared with the weight of holiness. Isaiah was wrecked. Undone. He was not alone in this experience. Fear and trembling were common among people who saw God. Not God as they imagined him to be but God as he really is.

When Job, a righteous man, encounters God, he says, "I had heard of you . . . but now my eye sees you; therefore I despise myself, and repent in dust and ashes."[4] When Manoah catches a glimpse of God, he says to his wife, "We shall surely die, for we have seen God."[5] As the glory of the Lord appears to the shepherds, they become "sore afraid."[6] After Jesus reveals a glimpse of his power and authority by providing a miraculous catch of

---

2. Isa. 9:6.
3. Isa. 6:1–5.
4. Job 42:5–6.
5. Judg. 13:22.
6. Luke 2:9 KJV.

fish, Simon Peter says to him, "Depart from me, for I am a sinful man, O Lord."[7]

Notably, the Lord never corrects anyone for responding in this way, as if they are taking their religion too seriously. If anything, they (and we) don't take God seriously enough.

Commenting on the anemic, awe-less expressions of mainstream Christianity, Annie Dillard bemoans our lack of appreciation for the more ominous, less safe aspects of God. "On the whole," she writes, "I do not find Christians, outside of the catacombs, sufficiently sensible of conditions. Does anyone have the foggiest idea what sort of power we so blithely invoke? Or, as I suspect, does no one believe a word of it? . . . It is madness to wear ladies' straw hats and velvet hats to church; we should all be wearing crash helmets. Ushers should issue life preservers and signal flares; they should lash us to our pews."[8]

God's holiness is his only attribute that the Bible repeats three times. He is not just "holy" but "holy, holy, holy." Whenever we see repetition in the Bible, it is good to envision several bold-printed exclamation points at the end of the sentence. In biblical language, repetition always conveys emphatic force. King David cries "Absalom, Absalom" in grief over his estranged, deceased son. Jesus cries "Martha, Martha" with tender concern about her restlessness. He cries "Jerusalem, Jerusalem" to those who have denied him, yet whom he longs to bring under his care. Each twofold repetition represents a deep stirring of the heart. But when the thrice-holy God shows up, it shakes the earth.

With no desire to pick on those who wear straw and velvet

---

7. Luke 5:8.
8. Annie Dillard, *Teaching a Stone to Talk* (New York: Harper Perennial, 2013), 58.

hats, Annie Dillard is still on to something. It may be more appropriate to wear a crash helmet to church.

Let's not forget that the angels in Isaiah's vision are morally perfect. Yet even in their perfection, they cover their faces—a standard reflex to feeling unworthy—when God is in view. Why is this so? Because God's holiness is his *superlativeness* in all things and over all other beings, including perfect angelic ones.[9] His holiness is the sum of his attributes and his awesome perfection, wonder, grandeur, and worth.

God's better-than-ness dwarfs our trophies and promotions.

God's stronger-than-ness dwarfs our muscle and achievement.

God's God-ness dwarfs our perches of human pride.

I find it remarkable that the source of Isaiah's distress is his lips. We would expect a prophet to curse his own lips in the same way we might expect a scholar to curse her own intellect, a sprinter his own legs, a surgeon her own fingers, or a singer his own vocal cords. That is to say, we wouldn't expect it at all. Who looks down on and loathes their greatest strength? But compared with God's superlative holiness, the things we rely on most to provide a foundation for our lives—in Isaiah's case, his lips—are shaken along with the whole earth, which is filled with his glory, not ours.

Every fall, a new group of freshmen enrolls at Harvard. Many arrive as freshly minted high-school valedictorians. Most received perfect or near-perfect scores on their entrance exams. These exceptional students have always sat at the top of their classes, with plaques and certificates to prove it. But half of them must undergo a crisis when they discover that compared with their

---

9. I first heard the connection between God's holiness and his superlativeness in a sermon by Tim Keller.

newest peers, they are no longer exceptional. Even at Harvard, 50 percent of all students—past valedictorian titles, plaques, and perfect test scores notwithstanding—are now in the bottom half of their class.

Like Isaiah with his preacher's lips, we may live under an illusion that we, too, are superlative. If we enjoy relative success, we may feel that we are somehow different, unique, special, elite, better than. But a time will come when any illusions of a grandeur located in ourselves will be shattered. Eventually, we will encounter a superiority elsewhere that cuts us down to size. Even those who are used to winning will fall from their pedestals, if not by defeat then by attrition. How many of us know who the tenth US president was, who has won the most Grammy awards, or who invented paper? In one hundred years, most of the world's seven billion people will be forgotten, including the so-called winners. Our great-great-grandchildren will never hear our names uttered, let alone be aware of what we accomplished with our lives. In a hundred years? All new people.[10]

Ce❦❧

This search for self-esteem through religion and moral virtue presents a greater problem. No matter how good we have been and what we have done for God and others, there is always somebody whose relative goodness makes us feel less than.

According to an article in the *Berkshire Eagle*, John and Libby Moritz lost all three of their children in a car crash. In response to their grief, they founded a nonprofit for vulnerable children. They sponsored orphanages in Mexico and Grenada,

---

10. I once heard Anne Lamott answer the "In a hundred years?" question in this way.

provided scholarships in Kenya and India, alleviated hunger in the Philippines, and provided shoes in Guatemala. They bought a large farm and turned it into a foster home. In virtually everything, they became others-centered. They used their own money to fund the work. In the summers, John tended to his swimming-pool business. During off months, they visited the orphanages and programs they sponsored.

Unsurprisingly, the article about the Moritzes began, "Prepare to feel a little guilty. It's not that John and Libby Moritz would want anybody to feel guilty. It's just that if you want to compare good-deed checklists with them, yours will probably come up short."[11]

In her remarkable book about advent, Fleming Rutledge writes of a woman who lived in luxury who also prided herself on being a devout Christian. As Rutledge tells it, the woman absolved herself from guilt by declaring, "I don't think God wants me to be Mother Teresa." Rutledge responds, "Can we really get ourselves off the hook that way? Imagine you and me on judgment day, saying, 'Well, Lord, in November 1996 I put a box of Cheerios and a jar of peanut butter in a box at Saint John's . . .' As a character in a Barbara Pym novel says, 'The trouble with doing good works is that one can never be said to have done one's share . . .'[12] All we can say is, 'Lord, have mercy on me, a sinner.'"

Rutledge continues, "He who congratulates himself on having done enough is precisely the one who has not. He who thinks himself safe is in the greatest danger. The man who trembles to think of himself before the judgment seat is closer to the kingdom

---

11. Article by Timothy Q. Cebula, *Berkshire Eagle*, November 18, 1996, quoted in Fleming Rutledge, *Advent: The Once and Future Coming of Jesus Christ* (Grand Rapids: Eerdmans, 2018), 231.

12. Barbara Pym, *An Academic Question*, as quoted in Rutledge, *Advent*.

of heaven than the one who complacently assumes he is on the side of the angels . . . There is no human merit anywhere to bail us out."[13]

"Not everyone who says to me, 'Lord, Lord,' will enter the kingdom of heaven," Jesus said. "On that day many will say to me, 'Lord, Lord, did we not prophesy in your name, and cast out demons in your name, and do many mighty works in your name?' And then will I declare to them, 'I never knew you; depart from me, you workers of lawlessness.'"[14]

In a book that seeks to redeem the wearying voices of regret, hurt, and fear, is there a place for such sobering stories and statements? Don't they just amplify our weariness instead of relieving it? If you're feeling defeated, let me tell you there is a better way. We can get out of the tiresome, futile maze of do-better religion and be-better self-esteem.

Returning to Isaiah.

After the prophet is brought low by God's superlative holiness, after the foundations of the temple and his pulpit and life are shaken beneath him, after he forsakes any notion that his best deeds amount to anything more than filthy rags,[15] after silencing all boasting in his own virtue, pedigree, and gift package, the God who is holy, holy, holy begins rebuilding Isaiah with a new kind of esteem. Isaiah will not be able to find this esteem within himself. Instead, it will have to come from the outside. It will

---

13. Rutledge, *Advent*, 233–34.
14. Matt. 7:21–23.
15. Isa. 64:6.

be given freely to him by God, whose name is Holy and whose essence is Love.

As Isaiah prepares to die, an angel arrives with a blazing coal from the altar and places it on his unclean lips. The consuming fire of God heads directly to the source of Isaiah's unsanitary shame. But the fire does not cremate his lips. It does not reduce him to dust. Instead, it purifies just as fire purifies a precious metal—melting away the dross to shape the metal into something useful, lovely, even priceless.

Isaiah takes note that the hem of God's robe filled the temple with glory.[16] There is another place in Scripture that features the hem of a robe. This time, it is the hem of Jesus' robe, which was pregnant with healing powers for a woman who had suffered twelve years from incurable bleeding. Having spent her life savings on doctors to no avail, she approaches Jesus in desperation. She breaks through the crowd, falls to the ground, and grasps the hem of his robe. Power goes out from Jesus, and instantly she is healed. Jesus turns to her—to the woman who had come to him only as a last resort—and says, "Daughter, your faith has made you well; go in peace."[17]

"Truly, I say to you, if you have faith like a grain of mustard seed, you will say to this mountain, 'Move from here to there,' and it will move, and nothing will be impossible for you."[18]

When Jesus spoke these words, I don't think he was talking about literal mountains. There is an even bigger mountain that the tiniest bit of faith can move—the mountain of a human heart. It is the mountain of Jesus-as-last-resort, the hem of whose

---

16. Isa. 6:1.
17. Luke 8:43–48.
18. Matt. 17:20.

robe never crosses our minds until we have exhausted every other option. It is the mountain that moves when we pray at long last "God, have mercy on me, the sinner" and "Woe is me, for I am a [wo]man of unclean lips" and "Forgive us our debts."

The greatest mountain to be moved is a needy, tired heart that won't run to Jesus except as a last resort. All you need is nothing; all you need is need.[19]

The thing God wants most from you is an admission of your not-enough-ness. God ignores your moral-virtue resume because his deeper concern is not what you can do for him but what he can do for you. God is tuned in to the worst things about you and still loves you. You are exposed before his holy, haunting gaze—down to the core where your darkest secrets and vilest motives lie—and he does not reject you. If the most trusted person in your life told you that all these things are true, would you believe it? Would it change things for you?

Would it change *you*?

Once I received a call in the middle of the night from a woman in our church. She wanted me to know that her husband and the father of her children, Richard,[20] was at home alone, high on a cocktail of oxycodone and Xanax and whiskey, with a loaded pistol nearby. I knew what this meant, so I got into my car and drove to their home. Richard answered the door in a stupor, and we sat down to talk. I asked him how he was doing, and he told me that he hated himself and he knew that God hated him, too.

---

19. I first heard this phrase in a sermon by Tim Keller.
20. "Richard" is not his real name.

It doesn't take an opium addiction, alcoholism, or family failure for us to think this way about ourselves and about God. Like the sheriff in Cormac McCarthy's *No Country for Old Men*, we limp through life in quiet despondency as we think to ourselves, "I always thought when I got older that God would sort of come into my life in some way. He didn't. I don't blame him. If I was him I'd have the same opinion about me that he does."[21]

It was my sacred privilege to look Richard in the eye and tell him that in the trenches of that very moment, and beyond the shadow of any doubt, God does not hate him—which is why he must not hate himself. "Be careful, Richard," I said. "It is a grievous thing to hate a child whom God cannot stop loving."

He looked at me as if I were cross-eyed, but also with a last-ditch desperation to hear more.

I told Richard about Isaiah in the temple, the unclean lips, the woes and the self-loathing, and the coal. I told him about the fire of God that does not cremate us in our places of shame but instead refines, purifies, and makes beauty out of what's ugly. We then turned to Jesus' parable of the father who couldn't stop loving his two sons—one a hedonistic, self-centered prodigal and the other a resentful, holier-than-thou "saint." When the prodigal returns home after humiliating the family, wishing his father dead, and squandering half of the family's wealth on sex and self, before any apologies or restitution are offered the father lifts his robe, exposing the hem—yes, the hem—and runs toward his busted-up, self-loathing son with a bold, hard-hugging welcome.

Richard permitted me to fly him to Arizona and help him admit himself into rehab. Over time, he maintained his sobriety, moved back home to his wife and children, and later became an

---

21. Cormac McCarthy, *No Country for Old Men* (New York: Vintage, 2006), 267.

elder in our church. To this day, he is one of the best shepherds to Christ's sheep I've had the honor of serving alongside. Beautiful people don't just happen.

Richard doesn't hate himself anymore. He couldn't if he tried, because he has come to see that even when he was at his worst, God could not stop loving him.

How about you? Would you dare to believe that God does not hate you? That he sees you at your worst and loves you no less? That if you confess your sins, sorrows, and fears to him right now, you will not be cremated but healed? Would you dare see the fiery coal of God not as a threat that will dangle you over hell but as a cure coming straight from the heart of heaven? Would you dare to believe that God does not expect you to meet him on the level of his superlativeness (not possible) but wants only to meet you on the ground where the hem of his robe awaits you? Would you dare believe that your own regret, hurt, and fear— your not-enough-ness—is not a barrier to God's healing mercy but the very occasion for it?

As Dane Ortlund has observed, our "regions of deepest shame and regret are not hotels through which divine mercy passes but homes in which divine mercy abides . . . our sins do not cause [God's] love to take a hit. Our sins cause his love to surge forward all the more."[22]

If you are a Christian, I hope you will think of the coal whenever the bread and wine of communion touch your lips. Like a coal from the altar, these are meant to be received like a kiss.

And if ever you're tempted to hate yourself, be careful.

It is a grievous thing to hate a child whom God cannot stop loving.

---

22. Dane Ortlund, *Gentle and Lowly* (Wheaton, IL: Crossway, 2020), 179–80.

THE GRAND CANYON

In January 2007, a famous violinist took his $3.5 million Stradivarius onto the platform of a Washington, D.C., subway and started playing free music. Dressed incognito in jeans, a T-shirt, and a ballcap, Joshua Bell—accustomed to playing for packed concert halls and world leaders and getting paid $1,000 per minute—brought his best in a forty-three-minute solo concert for a total of 1,097 passersby. According to camera footage, only seven people stopped to listen. A few others gave money without stopping, totaling $32 and change. The remaining 1,070 people rushed by, barely noticing what was going on, and went about their day.[1]

It is remarkable how easily we can miss beauty, even when it is right in front of us.

Sometimes we miss beauty because we choose to look the other way. When I was a child, my parents drove more than five hundred miles to show me the Grand Canyon. When we arrived, despite my mother's pleading, I refused to get out of the car and look. There were two reasons why. First, I resented the canyon because it took me away from Saturday-morning cartoons. Second, the comic book I brought with me seemed more

---

1. Gene Weingarten, "Pearls before Breakfast: Can One of the Nation's Great Musicians Cut through the Fog of a D.C. Rush Hour? Let's Find Out," *Washington Post*, accessed April 8, 2007, www.washingtonpost.com/lifestyle/magazine/pearls -before-breakfast-can-one-of-the-nations-great-musicians-cut-through-the-fog-of-a -dc-rush-hour-lets-find-out/2014/09/23/8a6d46da-4331-11e4-b47c-f5889e061e5f_story .html?itid=lk_inline_manual_4.

interesting at the time. My parents didn't force me to participate. Instead, they enjoyed the scenery without me for three long, irritating hours. I faintly remember my father saying to my mother, "He will regret this someday, and that will be his punishment."

How true this is, that we miss out on the best things because we prefer the lesser things. We miss out on the wondrous things because we prefer the humdrum things. We miss out on the adventure because we prefer the safe, contained, controllable things. Gazing at beauty is its own reward. Looking away from beauty is its own punishment.

I have not been back to the Grand Canyon. In hindsight, I wish I had looked.

Other times, things that are beautiful don't move us because our senses are numbed and our hearts callused from sorrow. What good is a Rembrandt painting, a Mozart score, or an ocean view when we are wracked with pain? What good is loveliness when our lives are unraveling? As Camus once said, "Beauty is unbearable, drives us to despair, offering us for a minute the glimpse of an eternity that we should like to stretch out over the whole of time. I can barely conceive of a beauty in which there is no Melancholy."[2]

When Job and his wife received news that their ten children had been assaulted and killed, she turned to him and mocked his faith. "Do you still hold fast your integrity? Curse God and die."[3] Most of us will not suffer to the extent that Job and his wife did. But that does not diminish the dreadfulness of our own hard battles.

Whether now or later, our hearts are bound to get blistered by grief.

---

2. Albert Camus, *Carnets: 1935–1942* (London: Hamish Hamilton, 1963).
3. Job 2:9.

C. S. Lewis honestly expressed what many of us feel but hesitate to say out loud. "When you are happy," he wrote, "so happy you have no sense of needing [God], so happy that you are tempted to feel His claims upon you as an interruption, if you remember yourself and turn to Him with gratitude and praise, you will be—or so it feels—welcomed with open arms. But go to Him when your need is desperate, when all other help is vain, and what do you find? A door slammed in your face, and a sound of bolting and double bolting on the inside. After that, silence. You may as well turn away. The longer you wait, the more emphatic the silence will become . . . Why is He so present a commander in our time of prosperity and so very absent a help in time of trouble?"[4]

One time in my midtwenties, I had it out with God. I'd been out of town visiting a friend and called my wife to tell her I was on my way home. Strangely, the "Hello?" on the other line came not from her but from a teenager.

"Is Patti there?" I asked awkwardly.

"No," the teenager responded. "She had an accident, and my mom has taken her to the hospital. I was asked to stay here until my mom returns."

"What happened to Patti?"

"I have no idea," he said.

That was before we had mobile phones. With no way to get in touch with Patti or of knowing what had happened to her or how serious it was, I got in the car and began what was supposed to be a four-hour drive that became seven hours because of a traffic jam that began around mile four. Filled with fear and rage, I began screaming obscenities at the God who is love and who is sovereign

4. C. S. Lewis, *A Grief Observed* (New York: HarperOne, 1999), Kindle.

over all things. It would serve no good purpose for me to tell you exactly what I said in my raging prayer. All I'll say is that it was more insulting than what Job's wife said to Job about God.

After I calmed down, I got scared. I began to wonder if God would strike me with lightning or something worse. Perhaps he would break through the clouds, sew my mouth shut, sit me down, and give me a speech like the one he gave to Job after Job accused him of mocking the despair of the innocent.[5] From inside Job's custom-made hurricane, God answered, "Who is this that darkens counsel by words without knowledge? Dress for action like a man; I will question you . . . Where were you when I laid the foundation of the earth? Tell me, if you have understanding . . . Shall a faultfinder contend with the Almighty? He who argues with God, let him answer . . . Will you even put me in the wrong? Will you condemn me that you may be in the right? Have you an arm like God, and can you thunder with a voice like his?"[6]

God did not strike me with lightning. Nor did he sew my lips shut or confront me with a scathing speech. Instead, he got me home to my wife, who was safe and sound when I arrived.

The world is both exquisite and terrible.

At its best, the world bears constant witness to the God who "is a Spirit, infinite, eternal, and unchangeable, in his being, wisdom, power, holiness, justice, goodness, and truth."[7] And yet, distracted and afflicted by the world's terrors, it is easy to miss the music that comes to us free of charge. Who has time for God when there are people to please, politicians to criticize, addictions to feed, holes to dig ourselves out of, and pandemics

---

5. Job 9:23.
6. See Job 38–40 for the full speech.
7. *Westminster Shorter Catechism*, answer to question 1, "What is God?"

to navigate? Who has use for God when the life he gives us turns out to be unstable and wretched?

Even if our lives seem trouble free, we remain numb to God because when left to ourselves, we cannot see him clearly. Like the 1,070 souls who were ambivalent toward a musical master-piece in the D.C. subway, the unaided human heart is the same toward the Master and Maker of all things. We walk on by, numb to the brilliance and beauty right in front of us. For this reason, the apostle Paul prayed earnestly for his friends "that the God of our Lord Jesus Christ, the Father of glory, may give [them] the Spirit of wisdom and of revelation in the knowledge of him, hav-ing the eyes of [their] hearts enlightened, that [they] may know what is the hope to which he has called [them], what are the riches of his glorious inheritance in the saints, and what is the immeasurable greatness of his power toward us who believe."[8]

In simple terms, Paul prayed that they (and we) would be able to see what cannot be seen without the intervening help of God—namely, God.

The hard truth is that no person can love God until they see God, and no person can see God until God gifts them with his Spirit.[9] And yet the wonderful truth is that God *does* gift his Spirit liberally, opening the eyes of human hearts to see and savor not only the glory that is presented to their senses (the sound of Joshua Bell, the sight of the Grand Canyon, the taste of ice cream, the texture of silk) but also a greater glory that is less

8. Eph. 1:17–19.
9. See John 3:1–8; Eph. 2:1–10; John 6:44, etc.

accessible to the senses, but no less real—the eternal glory of God. Remarkably, God's hidden glory shows up meaningfully in life's beauty as well as in life's suffering.

The apostle Paul, whose life and ministry were filled with trouble, reveals his appreciation for the hidden glory when he writes, "We rejoice in our sufferings, knowing that suffering produces endurance, and endurance produces character, and character produces hope, and hope does not put us to shame, because God's love has been poured into our hearts through the Holy Spirit who has been given to us."[10]

I cannot help but chuckle when people ask if I, a pastor, have ever had a job in the real world. I once heard another pastor answer the question by saying that he experiences more of the real world in one week than many do in a lifetime. He then reviewed the many distraught marriages, estranged parent-child relationships, financial train wrecks, addiction and adultery interventions, deaths, and suicide wreckage into which his work has called him. This part of a pastor's calling is heavy, but it is also a privilege. I say this because it is especially in the real-world troubles, when we're down on the ground in the dirt, grasping for the hem of Jesus' garment, that God opens our eyes to see him and know him more clearly. When God does this, we pastors are honored to have a front-row seat.

Not long ago, I received a note from a mother on the first anniversary of her teenage son's suicide. The previous year had been excruciating for her, her husband, and their other son. Touchingly and miraculously, her note was filled with a settled hope that had become a companion to her unspeakable grief. She spoke of a confidence that had been given to her by God

10. Rom. 5:3–5.

"that the sadness on this earth will only serve to intensify the joy of heaven." Every day she wears a bracelet with the word *tetelesthai* engraved on its outside, which is the Greek word Jesus cried from the cross meaning, "It is finished." She wears the bracelet to remind herself of what is true—that her young son, a sweet and kind and loyal believer in Jesus who tragically succumbed to self-harm in a moment of weakness, will not be judged by the last thing that he did before he died. Instead, he will be judged by the last thing Jesus did before *he* died as he cried, "Father, forgive them, for they know not what they do."[11]

The mother ended her note with the words "What comfort and such hope!" Along with her note came the gift of a wooden sign paraphrasing Tolkien, which sits in plain view on a bookshelf next to my desk. The sign reads, "All sad things become untrue."

There are many other real-world stories of people hoping against hope that I could tell you. These are frail people like you and me. The Spirit of God has been *given* to them, along with an ability to *see* with eyes of faith—a faith that is rooted in time-space history by Jesus' life, death, burial, resurrection, and coming return.

There was a widow who gifted to me her husband's "happy socks," which he wore as he fought terminal cancer to remind himself that his best days were still ahead of him in the new heaven and new earth.[12] I wear those socks every year on Easter to remind myself that what was true for him in his dying days is also true for me in my living ones.

There was also a woman whose oncologist told her that she had two weeks left. As I helped her plan her funeral, her prevailing

---

11. Luke 23:34.
12. Rev. 21:1–5.

emotion was joy. But like the mother who had lost her son, her joy in no way negated, diminished, or disrespected her accompanying sadness. To the contrary, her joy completed her sadness, and her sadness completed her joy. In staying awake to both emotions simultaneously, she showed herself to be fully human and fully alive, even in the shadow of death's dark valley.

It is a miracle that Jesus endured the cross of death "for the joy that was set before him."[13] It is also a miracle when other frail humans like ourselves can do the same.

We are told that when unspeakable tragedy struck Job and his wife, Job's impulse response—the one for which she despised him—was to fall on his knees and worship God, saying, "Naked I came from my mother's womb, and naked shall I return. The LORD gave, and the LORD has taken away; blessed be the name of the LORD."[14]

Having witnessed as much as I have while walking with people in the trenches as their pastor, I can tell you that when my next time of testing comes, I hope I won't curse or cuss at God. I hope that this time, my heart will contain in full measure whatever it was that caused a grieving mother to quote Tolkien about sad things coming untrue, a dying man to reach for his happy socks, a woman to be fully alive while she planned her own funeral, and Job to worship.

Thankfully, it seems, Job's wife found a way out of her cynicism and learned how to live again. You can read all about it in their story.

Perhaps we who have become cozy with cynicism can learn to live again, too?

---

13. Heb. 12:2.
14. Job 1:21.

FINE MOTOR SKILLS

There are practices that, when woven into the daily rhythms of life, can help us see God more clearly amid the beauty and terrors of life. Two such practices, *abiding* and *beholding*, are foundational to knowing God and experiencing his closeness, goodness, and glory. Abiding and beholding in God's presence can help us not only endure the weariness we experience from regret, hurt, and fear but even find joy and meaning within it. Together, abiding and beholding are like tilling and planting for a farmer. The farmer does the work he knows to do, but when the work is done, he is at the mercy of God for rain, sunlight, and harvest. Likewise, our souls must be carefully and daily tended to, even as we entrust ourselves to God for the growth.

First, abiding.

In his teaching about the day of judgment, Jesus told a parable about ten virgins. Five of them were wise, having filled their lamps with oil in case the bridegroom returns unexpectedly. The other five were foolish, not having tended to their lamps at all. When the bridegroom's arrival was announced, the foolish virgins panicked and begged the others to share their oil. The wise virgins answered, "Since there will not be enough for us and for you, go rather to the dealers and buy for yourselves." While the foolish virgins went scrambling to find oil, the bridegroom came and took the wise virgins with him to the wedding feast, and then shut the door. The foolish virgins returned and begged that the door be opened also to them. The bridegroom answered,

"Truly, I say to you, I do not know you." Jesus finished the teaching by saying, "Watch therefore, for you know neither the day nor the hour."[1]

It is notable that the bridegroom's (Jesus') word to the foolish and unprepared was not "I disapprove of you" or "Get your act together" or "I'm hurt and offended by your inaction." Instead, he said that he did not *know* them. They had not taken time to seek or nourish a relationship with him. This foolishness and lack of care revealed their hearts; they were far from him. They had no preparations—no oil for their lamps—and therefore no illuminating potential for dark times or places.

The prophet Amos compared this self-inflicted predicament to a famine, one that pertains not to a scarcity of food and drink but to a starving of the soul for lack of hearing the word of the Lord.[2] The apostle Paul called it conformity to the pattern of this world, the solution for which is to be transformed by the renewing of our minds, dwelling and *thinking* on whatever is pure, lovely, commendable, excellent, and praiseworthy.[3] The psalmist described such thinking as meditation—not the eastern version that involves emptying our minds but the Judeo-Christian version that involves filling our minds with Scripture's revealed attributes, thoughts, wisdom, warnings, and promises of God. To the degree that we orient our thoughts around these, God's treasures, we will be poised not only to withstand regret, hurt, and fear but even, by God's grace, to flourish in their presence. To the degree that we do not do so, we will subject ourselves to the worst and most costly kind of famine.

---

1. Matt. 25:1–13.
2. Amos 8:11.
3. Rom. 12:1–2; Phil. 4:8.

The anxious virgins in Jesus' parable are a cautionary tale for us. Their arrival at the banquet resembled wedding crashers looking for a party paid for by a stranger, versus true bridesmaids showing up for a bride and groom they had known and loved for many years.

While Jesus' primary focus in the parable is his second coming, when he "will come to judge the living and the dead,"[4] there is also a secondary but no less essential focus. Keeping our lamps filled with oil—a metaphor for ordering our lives around *knowing Jesus* through worship with a local church, regular Bible study, and prayer (what some call the formative "spiritual disciplines")—is imperative for survival when our day of darkness comes.

Commenting on how African American Christians have so often been able to forgive atrocious betrayals toward them and their communities, one writer says, "They are so practiced, through regular worship, Bible study, and prayer, that they don't need to run out to the store in the middle of the night to buy more oil. They've been in the middle of the night for a long time . . . to forgive . . . It's part of their DNA as a Christian community. They have been storing up oil for generations." As a case in point, the writer recalls the atrocious, senseless lethal shooting in 2015 at Charleston's Emanuel AME Church, which occurred during a Bible study. "When the church reopened for worship . . . one of the ministers said that people kept asking why, and how" friends and family could forgive the shooter. The minister said, "Those of us who know Jesus, we can look through the window of our faith, and we see hope, we see light."[5]

---

4. The Apostles' Creed.
5. Fleming Rutledge, *Advent: The Once and Future Coming of Jesus Christ* (Grand Rapids: Eerdmans, 2018), 98–99.

Later in this book, I will share candidly about my battle with anxiety and depression.[6] A friend who shares the same struggles urged me to memorize 2 Corinthians 10:4–5 so I could access it whenever the anxiety gremlins wage fresh assault. The passage reads, "The weapons of our warfare are not of the flesh but have divine power to destroy strongholds. We destroy arguments and every lofty opinion raised against the knowledge of God, and take every thought captive to obey Christ."[7]

If your story includes anxiety, you know what it is like to grow weary from meditating on imagined worst-case scenarios. I'm here to tell you, there is no sustained way to confront those scenarios without the presence of a steadily nourished, full reservoir of biblical truth. This reservoir can be formed only through ongoing minidecisions to say yes to daily Bible reading versus an extra half hour of sleep; yes to weekly church and group Bible study versus more hours of television and internet scrolling; yes to being present with and opening our checkbooks for God and others versus excessive *me* time and *me* pursuits; yes to denying ourselves, taking up our crosses daily, and following Jesus versus denying our neighbors, taking up our comforts, and following our dreams.

The practice of getting out of our anxious heads and into the life of God and neighbor via daily rhythms of exercising the "means of grace" has been a literal lifesaver for me. It has resourced me to confront "what if" scenarios with courage instead of helplessly replaying them or sweeping them under the rug. What if I go unemployed someday? What if someone attacks my reputation with a false accusation? What if people

---

6. Scott Sauls, *Befriend* (Wheaton, IL: Tyndale, 2016), 35–42.
7. 2 Cor. 10:4–5.

discover and publicize the worst things that I actually am guilty of thinking, saying, or doing? What if something terrible happens to someone I love? What if another pandemic happens? What if I inherit Alzheimer's from my mother?

In each such instance, the practice of "filling my lamp with oil" through consistent rhythms of faith prepares me to face every "what if." What if the worst-case scenario does happen? If it does, it will be sad for the time being. But long term, in a hundred and a thousand and a million years from now, the *worst* case scenario for a believer will not include death, mourning, crying, or pain.[8] The long-term *worst* case scenario is that all sad and hurtful things will come untrue. Just as certain as Christ's empty tomb is this: We too will rise from death's dark into a world where every day will be better than the one before. World without end. Amen.

Maybe this is why Black Church hymns and spirituals are uniquely saturated with lyrics about the life to come.

Don't underestimate the power of formative habit. What you take into you is what will come out of you when the days of trouble come. As Annie Dillard famously said, "How we spend our days is, of course, how we spend our lives. What we do with this hour, and that one, is what we are doing. A schedule defends from chaos and whim. It is a net for catching days. It is a scaffolding on which a worker can stand and labor . . . a mock-up of reason and order . . . it is a peace and a haven set into the wreck of time; it is a lifeboat on which you find yourself, decades later, still living."[9]

The wreck of time. That Annie Dillard. She has such a way with words.

---

8. Rev. 21:1–5.

9. Annie Dillard, *The Writing Life* (New York: Harper Collins, 2009), Kindle.

Tend to your lamp. Fill it to the brim with oil each day. Turn an unopened Bible into a well-worn Bible, for "a Bible that's falling apart usually belongs to someone who isn't."[10] Engage all the practices that will help you draw near to Jesus, not merely to know about him but to *know* him. Don't become a wedding crasher who could have prepared but didn't. Abiding in Christ, who is the light of the world, is your safeguard from getting lost in the dark.

Second, beholding.

To behold means to notice, to commit our attention to, to discard all clutter to focus on one thing. As King David once prayed, "The LORD is my light and my salvation; whom shall I fear? The LORD is the stronghold of my life; of whom shall I be afraid? . . . though war arise against me, yet I will be confident. *One thing* have I asked of the LORD, that will I seek after: that I may dwell in the house of the LORD all the days of my life, to gaze upon the beauty of the LORD and to inquire in his temple."[11]

David's awareness of his Creator, whose beauty carries more weight than the weight of the whole world, helped him face tragic, temporal realities. The one thing he sought every day in the temple (aka in "church"), the one thing that became his non-negotiable that he could not live without, was a daily, fixed gaze in the direction of God.

The apostle Paul also saw the weight of God's glory as *the*

---

10. This quote is often attributed to Charles Haddon Spurgeon. Original source unknown.

11. Ps. 27:1–4, emphasis mine.

essential focus to make all forms of weariness feel weightless in comparison. He writes, "We do not lose heart . . . We are afflicted in every way . . . perplexed . . . persecuted . . . struck down . . . given over to death . . . [but] knowing that he who raised the Lord Jesus will raise us also with Jesus and bring us with you into his presence . . . For this *light momentary* affliction is preparing for us an *eternal weight of glory* beyond all comparison, as we look not to the things that are seen but to the things that are unseen. For the things that are seen are transient, but the things that are unseen are eternal."[12]

The prophet Isaiah gained hope and resolve to face the many hardships God promised would lie ahead of him. He, too, saw and savored the weight of God's glory that filled the temple (church), and through the temple, his own heart. As you read his book, you will see that as time goes by, two things grow in unison. First, his situation becomes increasingly dire. Second, his hope in God becomes increasingly amplified, along with his joy.

What specifically did David and Paul and Isaiah see when they beheld the glory of the Lord? Is it available to us? When our hearts' eyes are opened and our lamps filled with oil, the answer becomes yes.

The first thing to behold is the weight of God's grandeur, which can be accessed by looking around and looking up. David prays elsewhere, "O Lord, our Lord, how majestic is your name in all the earth! You have set your glory above the heavens . . . When I look at your heavens, the work of your fingers, the moon and the stars, which you have set in place, what is man that you are mindful of him, and the son of man that you care for him?"[13]

---

12. 2 Cor. 4:1–18, emphases mine.
13. Ps. 8:1–4.

About the work of God's fingers. What David notices as he beholds the glory of creation—the earth, moon, sun, stars, galaxies, and everything in them—is that God made it happen with mere fine motor skills. We use our fingers to write notes, brush hair out of our eyes, tie a shoe, scratch an itch, floss teeth. But God?

God uses *his* fingers to create, sustain, and govern square inches as well as whole continents, heads of hair as well as whole populations, tiny particles as well as unseen galaxies.

I once heard a preacher say that if the distance between earth and the sun (approximately 92 million miles) was reduced to the thickness of a sheet of paper, then the distance between earth and the nearest star would be a stack of papers seventy feet high, and the diameter of the galaxy would be a stack 310 miles high. And yet the galaxy—*our* galaxy—is merely a speck of dust in the universe. The famous astronomer Carl Sagan also noted the mindblowing immensity of the universe in his remarks about a satellite image of the earth caught inside a ray from the sun which he referred to as "the pale blue dot."

Sagan wrote, "Look again at that dot. That's here. That's home. That's us. On it everyone you love, everyone you know, everyone you ever heard of, every human being who ever was, lived out their lives. The aggregate of our joy and suffering, thousands of confident religions, ideologies, and economic doctrines, every hunter and forager, every hero and coward, every creator and destroyer of civilization, every king and peasant, every young couple in love, every mother and father, hopeful child inventor and explorer, every teacher of morals, every corrupt politician, every 'superstar,' every 'supreme leader,' every saint and sinner in the history of our species lived there—on a mote of dust suspended in a sunbeam. The earth is a very small stage in a vast cosmic arena."

Then Sagan drove home his point with brutal force: "Our posturings, our imagined self-importance, the delusion that we have some privileged position in the Universe, are challenged by this point of pale light. Our planet is a lonely speck in the great enveloping cosmic dark. In our obscurity, in all this vastness, there is no hint that help will come from elsewhere to save us from ourselves."[14]

There is no hint. Or is there?

What is man that you are mindful of him? Answering his own question, the psalmist David continues, "You have made him a little lower than the heavenly beings and crowned him with glory and honor. You have given him dominion over the works of your hands; you have put all things under his feet . . . O LORD, our Lord, how majestic is your name in all the earth!"[15]

In all the earth. Do you hear what's being said here? The earth—the tiny, pale blue dot in God's expansive universe—is also center stage for the manifestation of God's glory. Though small in size, planet Earth is nonetheless the only known place in the galaxies where God has included life in the landscape. And he created *us* to live here. The God of glory, it turns out, is also the God of small people, places, and things.

Another thing to behold is the weight of God's *condescending attentiveness* to you. By condescending, I don't mean the belittling or better-than-thou kind, but the caring and compassionate, down on your level, hem of the garment, and humble kind. Not the large and in-charge kind, but the kind that led Jesus, though

---

14. Carl Sagan, *Pale Blue Dot* (New York: Ballantine, 2011), Kindle.
15. Ps. 8:5–9.

he was in nature God, not to consider equality with God something to be grasped but to make himself nothing, taking the form of a servant—*your* servant.[16] His aim in doing so was (and still is) to tend to your weariness by descending to the ground beside you.

Jesus, the Maker of the moon and the stars, stoops to wash your dirty, tired, demoralized feet.[17]

✦

This is beholding. When God opens your eyes to help you see him, remember this: One of the main things he wants you to notice is that *he* notices and attends to *you*. By the work of his fingers, he knit you together in your mother's womb and declared that you are fearfully and wonderfully made. Yes, you—in all your frailty, doubt, and fear—remain the work of a Wonderful Counselor. He is so attentive to you that he knows your every motive and plan.

He searches you to *know* you. He is acquainted with all your ways. He knows your every thought before you think it, your every word before you speak it.

His thoughts of you are precious and countless. His is the name above every name, and yet he calls you by name.[18]

He is the man of sorrows, acquainted with grief, and yet he stores your tears in a bottle, calling them precious.[19]

He wore a crown of thorns on his head, while carefully numbering the hairs on yours.[20]

---

16. Phil. 2:5–8.
17. John 13:1–17.
18. Isa. 43:1.
19. Ps. 56:8.
20. Luke 12:7.

He was cursed and died upon a tree, and he sees you beneath a tree.[21]

He is the Ancient of Days who has numbered your days, authoring them in his book, before any of them came to be.[22]

The Maker of the moon and stars does not look at us from a bird's eye or satellite view. Instead, he stoops down to us, and even lower still, becoming small enough to inhabit a manger, grow up in a home without money or opportunity, and hail from an obscure, disregarded town from an insignificant region on the pale blue dot.

Can anything good come from Nazareth?

There in Nazareth and in the region of Galilee, he lived. Later, in Jerusalem, he suffered and died, and then he rose again in power, appeared to his disciples, ascended into heaven, and sent his Spirit so ordinary folk like us can get in on the glory. When the resurrected Jesus stood among his disciples, he said to the one who doubted him most, "Put your finger here [His finger! Can you hear the irony?]; see my hands. Reach out your hand and put it into my side. Stop doubting and believe." Thomas said to him, "My Lord and my God!" Then Jesus told him, "Because you have seen me, you have believed; blessed are those who have not seen and yet have believed."[23]

What remains is that Jesus will come again—this time not to defeated followers in a remote region but in unmistakable power and a glory so weighty and expansive, and with the inauguration of a future so bright, that it makes a dying man want to wear happy socks.

---

21. John 1:48.
22. Ps. 139:1–24.
23. John 20:26–29 NIV.

There is glory in the skies. Can you see it?
There is bread and wine on the table. Can you taste it?
There is a warm towel around your feet. Can you feel it?
There is free music on the platform. Can you hear it?

WHY WE SING

Has it ever seemed strange to you that people of faith sing together?

Besides at concerts and in bars, people singing together can seem awkwardly out of place. This is especially true if singing is not their area of expertise. If a group of accountants burst into song about the glories of math, or a football team about the wonders of shoulder pads, or culinary students about the riches of butter, most would assume that the singers have lost their minds. What makes singing to and about God any different, especially when so much *congregational* singing is done off key? Most of us are not professional singers, yet here we are, lifting up our voices in song. Why is singing together in this way, where a joyful noise is just as acceptable as exquisite harmonies, such a central part of what Christians do?[1] Why is it considered more normal than weird?

Christians sing for many reasons. One is because we recognize God as an artist and ourselves as creatives made in his image. When we express ourselves creatively, we honor our Maker and affirm our humanity. Paintings reveal the glory of their painters as the heavens reveal the glory of God.[2] Statues reveal the genius of their sculptors as human bodies reveal the genius of their God.[3] Literature and poetry reveal the inner life of their writers as Scripture reveals the inner life of God. As

---

1. Ps. 100:1.
2. Ps. 19:1.
3. Ps. 139:14.

a master wordsmith, God inspired the biblical writers as they inscribed poetry, wise sayings, and the epic drama of creation, fall, redemption, and glory. In the gospel narratives, also inspired by God, Jesus is revealed as the Warrior who saves us by slaying the dragon, the Prince who rescues and marries us, and the Beauty who kisses the beast in us all. Jesus takes center stage as the Hero in the happily-ever-after Fairy Tale that is also true.

As the Master Artist, God is also a composer of music. Many of the psalms begin with the headline "For the director of music." They are God's lyrical prototype, and melody is his delivery mechanism for joyful noises that move, inspire, and compel us to love and serve him, each other, and our neighbors. Music is a universally accessible love language and centerpiece of all peoples, places, and cultures. It is meaningful because it instructs us while also moving us. Life-giving lyrics inform our minds, but when put to song, they engulf and enflame our hearts. It is one thing to read the words of Isaiah 9 about a child being born and a son being given whose name shall be called Wonderful Counselor, Mighty God, Everlasting Father, and Prince of Peace.[4] It is quite another to hear these same biographical truths about Jesus put to music in Handel's symphonic masterpiece *Messiah*.

As Nietzsche astutely observed, "Music is a moral law. It gives soul to the universe, wings to the mind, flight to the imagination, a charm to sadness, and life to everything. It is the essence of order, and leads to all that is good, just and beautiful, of which it is the invisible, but nevertheless dazzling, passionate, and eternal form."[5]

---

4. Isa. 9:6.

5. *Wordsworth Dictionary of Musical Quotations* (Cody, WY: Wordsworth, 1991), 45. This saying is often attributed to Plato, although no original source has been identified.

C. S. Lewis, who early in his Christian life got irritated by the practice of singing in church, later changed his tune (pun intended) and affirmed how we "delight to praise what we enjoy because the praise not merely expresses but completes the enjoyment . . . the delight is incomplete until it is expressed . . . if one could really and fully praise [anything] to perfection—utterly 'get out' in poetry or music or paint the upsurge of appreciation which almost bursts you . . . indeed the object would be fully appreciated and our delight would have attained perfect development."[6]

In our singing, we delight in the goodness, beauty, love, and excellencies of God. We also delight in and spur on one another's enrichment and flourishing, as Paul affirms in his letter to the church at Ephesus: "Be filled with the Spirit, addressing *one another* in psalms and hymns and spiritual songs, singing and making melody to the Lord with your heart, giving thanks always and for everything to God the Father in the name of our Lord Jesus Christ."[7]

Why go on a rabbit trail about music?

What relevance does singing have for a book about regret, hurt, fear, and the weariness that they create?

The answer is, "Everything." Redeeming the voices that weary us requires that the volume be turned down on lies that suggest God resents us, he is ambivalent toward our sorrows, and he will not come through for us in the end. Turning the volume down on such lies requires turning the volume up on the truths

---

6. C. S. Lewis, *Reflections on the Psalms* (New York: HarperOne, 2017), Kindle.

7. Eph. 5:18–20, emphasis mine.

that put regret, hurt, and fear in proper perspective. To help us with this, God has provided the gift of song. What is true for athletes in a stadium, performers on a stage, mothers in a delivery room, and children who are learning to swim is also true of every Christian who is contending with what ails us. Sometimes we need a "holy roar"[8] from our Christian mentors and peers to inspire and empower us in the saving health of Christ. That roar can be heard most clearly and felt most deeply when we gather to sing.

Regret. Regret often stems from the guilt of our past. When John Newton was wearied with guilt from his many years working as a violent, cold-hearted slave trader, he wrote of an amazing grace that saved a wretch like him. Since then, "Amazing Grace" has been translated into an estimated fifty languages, has been performed an estimated ten million times, and has become the most widely sung piece of music the world has ever known. Remarkably, some of the most impactful renditions of the former slave trader's hymn have come from Black congregations—to whom we also owe a debt of gratitude for an archive of spirituals that help God's people faithfully lament injustice, contend for justice, and long for heaven.

In composing music that spoke grace to his own guilt and regret, Newton also tapped into a deep human need that is felt by victims as well as their perpetrators, injured parties as well as those who have done the injuring, those who have felt wretched pain and those who have committed wretched offenses. This universal need is to know that no matter how deep or dark the memory of sins—ones committed by us *and* ones committed

---

8. I first heard this terminology from Darren Whitehead and Chris Tomlin, who cowrote a book about worship by the same title.

against us—any broken, contrite, and penitent soul can be forgiven and redeemed through Jesus. "Amazing grace, how sweet the sound that saved a wretch like me. I once was lost but now am found. Was blind but now I see."

Hurt. Soon after Horatio Spafford received the news that his daughters had died in a shipwreck at sea, he composed a hymn that, like "Amazing Grace," has comforted generations of sufferers across the globe ever since. The hymn begins, "When peace like a river attendeth my way, when sorrows like sea billows roll, whatever my lot, thou hast taught me to say, 'It is well, it is well with my soul.'" Somehow, a mere journal entry or sermon was not sufficient to carry Spafford through the dark well of his grief. As the words came out of him, it also felt necessary for him to put "It Is Well" to music.

For as long as I have been a pastor, I have noticed that every time we sing "It Is Well" in church, the ones who sing the loudest are the sufferers. These include parents whose children are disabled or have died, men and women who have been abandoned by a spouse, people who experience chronic pain, illness, anxiety, or depression, those who are contending with a terminal diagnosis, widows and widowers, and many others. The first time I witnessed a person dying was when a thirty-five-year-old man with cancer asked those around his hospital bed to sing "It Is Well" over him as he passed. A single mother whose child died in a tragic accident asked the same from her pastors, family, and friends as they came alongside her in her grief. As people plan funerals for themselves and their loved ones, "It Is Well" almost always makes the list of songs requested—right alongside the twenty-third psalm. In their darkest moments, God's people want the truth about life, death, resurrection, and heaven not only to be read and spoken to them but also sung over them. Horatio Spafford will never know how much hope his own dark hour has brought to other sufferers.

Or perhaps he will.

Fear. When George Matheson began losing his eyesight in his twenties, his fiancée canceled their engagement because she could not imagine being married to a blind man. His loving sister stepped in as his caregiver for a time. But she, too, would eventually leave him to get married to start a family of her own. Left alone and in the dark with none but the invisible God to tend to his needs, Matheson despaired of his bleak future. In answer to his fears, and in less than five minutes with no editing, God gave him the words and music to "O Love That Will Not Let Me Go," another hymn that has since calmed the fears and worries of millions. The third stanza is especially and paradoxically powerful, which says, "Oh joy that seekest me through pain, I cannot close my heart to thee. I trace the rainbow through the rain, and feel the promise is not vain, that morn [heaven] shall tearless be."

Forgiveness for the past, strength for the present, and hope for the future. Three inestimable gifts to sing of and savor because of the finished work of Jesus Christ, our only comfort in life and in death. Time-tested hymns like these have provided steady anchors for centuries and will continue to do so for centuries to come. "Oh come, let us sing to the LORD; let us make a joyful noise to the rock of our salvation! Let us come into his presence with thanksgiving; let us make a joyful noise to him with songs of praise! For the LORD is a great God, and a great King above all gods."[9] Amen.

---

9. Ps. 95:1–3.

There are healing properties to music, especially the music of God.

Remarkably, God goes out of his way to love us out of our distress with songs of grace, comfort, and hope. Because God is gracious, this includes even the distress we have brought upon ourselves.

When the self-absorbed King Saul was tormented by an evil spirit, the young David would come in and play harp music for him. Whenever David did this, Saul relaxed and felt better, and the evil spirit was exorcised.[10]

When God's people felt distress over the coming judgment triggered by their own rebellion, the God whom they had forsaken wooed them tenderly back into his arms with a love song. "Sing aloud, O daughter of Zion; shout, O Israel! Rejoice and exult with all your heart . . . The LORD has taken away the judgments against you . . . you shall never again fear evil . . . The LORD your God is in your midst, a mighty one who will save; he will rejoice over you with gladness; he will quiet you by his love; he will exult over you with loud singing."[11]

In Jesus' famous parable about a father and his two sons, the prodigal asks for his inheritance early, which is the equivalent of wishing his father dead. The father grants his wish, and the son leaves home and spends every dime on wild living. Having wasted the full inheritance and bereft of any means for survival, the son went groveling home, armed with a carefully crafted

---

10. 1 Sam. 16:14–23.
11. Zeph. 3:14–17.

beggar's speech. "Father, I have sinned against heaven and before you," the son pleaded. "I am no longer worthy to be called your son. Treat me as one of your hired servants."

The prodigal son's speech contained two significant errors. The first was the idea that he had lost his worth, that he was "no longer worthy" to be called the father's son. Actually, the son had *never* earned his worth in the first place, just as we don't make ourselves worthy to be called God's daughters and sons based on any merit or virtue of our own. Being a daughter or son of God is a gift granted by his grace and mercy alone. It has nothing to do with our opinion of our worthiness. We are welcomed, embraced, and kept by him on our best days and our worst days, when we succeed and when we fail, when we love him and when we resent him, when we receive him and when we resist him, when we are pursuing him and when we are avoiding him. This is why he calls himself our Father, as opposed to our fair-weather friend. This is why he relates to us on the basis not of a contract but of a covenant.

God's love for us is consistent not because of the fickle goodness that is in us but because of the familial and fatherly goodness that is in him. Once we become heirs of his love through faith *in* Christ, nothing in all creation—including the things that we think, say, and do that make us feel ashamed—will ever be able to separate us from the love of God that is ours *through* Christ. In him, we will not be condemned because, in him, we cannot be condemned. "There is therefore now no condemnation for those who are in Christ Jesus."[12]

The son's second error was his belief that if the father did receive him back, it would have to be as a slave, not as a son.

---

12. Rom. 8:1, 38–39.

His newfound lack of entitlement is understandable. What father would welcome a harsh, hurtful, betraying prodigal back into the family? What brokenhearted father would risk having his heart broken again? What father would stop a prodigal in midspeech, be filled with compassion toward him, and run and embrace and kiss him, and do so *before* any reconciliation or repair has been offered? What father would then turn and say to the rest of the family and community, "Bring quickly the best robe, and put it on him, and put a ring on his hand, and shoes on his feet. And bring the fattened calf and kill it, and let us eat and celebrate"? What father would then entreat his other son, who still feels deeply burned by the injury and humiliation brought on the family by his backstabbing brother, to join the celebration?[13]

Our Father does all of this, and more.

This story is not just any story. It is *our* story, which has become part of God's Story of redeeming love through Christ. God *is* the Father in Jesus' parable, and we *are* his prodigals limping Home, fearful that he will not receive us back at all, yet hoping against hope that perhaps he will at least provide us with a cheap bunk in the slave quarters.

But when we return to him, we discover to our surprise that our Father runs out to us, embraces us, and ushers us back *Home*. When we come Home, we, too, are covered with a robe that is the robe of Jesus' righteousness. We, too, are given a ring that bears the signet and seal of belonging in the family of God. We, too, are given sandals to help us rise from our guilt, shame, and regret and then start limping, and then walking, and then running in our Father's strength, into our Father's house. For the Lord "gives power to the faint, and to him who has no might he increases

---

13. Luke 15:11–32.

strength. Even youths shall faint and be weary, and young men [including prodigals] shall fall exhausted; but they who wait for the LORD shall renew their strength; they shall mount up with wings like eagles; they shall run and not be weary; they shall walk and not faint."[14]

Then comes the lavish feast, prepared by our Father in celebration of our homecoming, and the whole village is invited. For there is more rejoicing at Home over one sinner who repents than over ninety-nine righteous persons who need no repentance.[15] If it was true back then, then it must still be true now. Though we may change, the Lord does not. Jesus Christ is the same yesterday, today, and forever.[16]

He cannot love you more and he will not love you less.[17]

There is nothing you will ever be able to do to change this.

---

14. Isa. 40:28–31.
15. Luke 15:7.
16. Mal. 3:6; Heb. 13:8.
17. I first heard this wonderful phrase from my friend and longtime mentor Scotty Smith.

BANANA BREAD

H ave you ever seen a bridesmaid faint at a wedding?

As a pastor, I have officiated many weddings. During rehearsal, I always warn those wearing high heels to keep their knees slightly bent while standing during the ceremony. The combination of heels and locked knees limits oxygen flow to the brain, which dramatically increases the possibility of fainting. Over the years, five bridesmaids have forgotten my instructions and fainted—once during singing, once during the exchange of rings, and three times during the vows. It makes for a memory, to be sure, but it's not a memory any bridesmaid wants to create.

Thankfully, I did not need to be the first responder in any of these fainting incidents. Each time, to my surprise, medical professionals from among the guests have left their seats and rushed toward the fallen bridesmaid to tend to her. Each time, they successfully resuscitated her, enabling us to finish the ceremony *with* the bridesmaid restored to her honored place, but now with her knees dutifully and carefully bent. At the end of the ceremony, when the last hymn is played and the bride and groom walk the aisle together, the bridesmaid sings. No longer fallen on the ground, she is also able to join the bride, groom, and guests for the dancing and feasting.

God's response to our sin is not unlike that of a medical professional to a fallen bridesmaid. Not only is it within his ability to awaken and restore us to our honored place, and not only is it within his ability to put a new song in our mouths,[1] it is also within his very nature to do so. With resolve, he gets out of his seat and tends to us on the ground where we have fallen. He breathes life into us as he tends to us in our weakest, most humiliating, and most vulnerable places. He lifts us up off the ground and invites us to sing of his love, step onto the dance floor, and take our honored seat at the marriage feast.

The psalmist describes these initiatives of God in Psalm 40: "I waited patiently for the LORD; he inclined to me and heard my cry. He drew me up from the pit of destruction, out of the miry bog, and set my feet upon a rock, making my steps secure. He put a new song in my mouth, a song of praise to our God . . . Blessed is the man who makes the LORD his trust . . . As for you, O LORD, you will not restrain your mercy from me; your steadfast love and your faithfulness will ever preserve me!"[2]

As we lie on the ground in our self-inflicted wounds and stupors, our Great Physician, Jesus, *intentionally* moves toward us, gets onto the ground with us, and breathes new life and hope into us. This is who he is, and this is what he does. His answer to our sin is not condemnation but grace. His answer to our shame is not rejection but tenderness. His answer to our repeat failures is not last-straw cancelation but never-ending embrace. His answer to our slowness to listen is not disgusted retreat but pursuing kindness. His answer to the grossest things about us is not to shout us down and shut us out but to quiet us with his love.[3]

This is not wishful thinking. I promise you it is not.

When Israel was languishing in exile and captivity because

---

1. Ps. 40:3.
2. Ps. 40:1–11.
3. Zeph. 3:17.

of their self-inflicted stupor of idolatry, sin, and guilt, Isaiah urged them to sing. Yes, to sing! "Sing, O barren one, who did not bear," said the Lord after they had insulted and abandoned him like a coldhearted, cheating wife.

When God gave these words to Israel, they were still living as prodigals in the far country. They had given their hearts fully to the false gods of surrounding pagan nations and embraced a lifestyle of illicit sex, love of money, and yearning for political power instead of God's power to sustain them. They had, like the prodigal son, prostituted themselves. As God's chosen bride, Israel had left her faithful, adoring Husband as she ran into the arms of other destructive lovers. Israel was so far gone and so far from Home that they could not fathom how to find their way back. They had given themselves over to the slavery in the midst of their deluded craving for what they thought would bring them freedom. Having forsaken the Lord as their Husband, they settled in with Babylon and Assyria as their lovers, even though both used and abused them repeatedly.

For fallen Israel, the words from Emily Dickinson's poem would have rung true: "I saw no way—The Heavens were stitched—I felt the Columns close . . . And back it slid—and I alone—A Speck upon a Ball."[4]

It is into this defeated, shame-ridden condition that God sends a hopeful, healing word to Israel through his prophet, Isaiah: "'Break forth into singing and cry aloud . . . Fear not, for you will not be ashamed . . . For your Maker is your husband . . . the LORD has called you like a wife deserted and grieved in spirit, like a wife of youth when she is cast off,' says your God . . . 'In

---

4. Emily Dickinson, "The heavens were stitched," 1830–1886 Poems, J378, Fr633, Houghton Library.

overflowing anger for a moment I hid my face from you, but with everlasting love I will have compassion on you,' says the LORD, your Redeemer."[5]

To intensify the point, God offered a similar word through another prophet, Hosea: "Behold, I will allure her . . . and speak tenderly to her . . . 'I will make you lie down in safety. And I will betroth you to me forever. I will betroth you to me in righteousness and in justice, in steadfast love and in mercy. I will betroth you to me in faithfulness. And you shall know the LORD.'"[6]

The message from the Lord to his unfaithful, adulterous, prodigal people is clear: He will never leave or forsake us. Though we are repeatedly unfaithful to him, he will never be unfaithful to us. Though he may withdraw his presence from us when we cheat on him with false and insufficient lovers such as sex, money, power, politics, and outrage, he will remain with us and true to us for better and for worse, in joy and in sorrow, in sickness and in health, as long as we live and into eternity.

As bridegroom to his bride, this is what our God does, because this is who our God is. Even when we are faithless, he will remain faithful. He will not disown us, because to do so would be to disown himself. And he cannot disown himself.[7]

❦

Have you ever stopped and marveled at how the Bible, including God's chosen family, is filled to the brim with screwups?

This is my favorite thing about the Bible. All the screwups

---

5. Isa. 54:1–8.
6. Hos. 2:14, 18–20.
7. 2 Tim. 2:13.

that are in there. It gives me hope, because if there is saving grace for wretches like them, then there must also be saving grace for wretches like me. In the next pages, I will share a few things about Abraham, Isaac, Jacob, Rahab, David, Peter, Paul, Mary Magdalene, and others that might make your skin crawl. Even though they are all considered heroes of the faith in the Bible and throughout the centuries, these heroes have also been horrific parents to their children, loveless toward their siblings, promiscuous in their bedrooms, liars and deceivers, adulterers and murderers, xenophobes and racists, blasphemous cowards and merciless aggressors. For further details, read on.

But for now, it is worth asking plainly why God chooses to do some of his best work through such bad, unsavory characters. Why wouldn't God choose to work through good people instead? Why wouldn't God use better ingredients to accomplish his purposes among women and men?

The simple answer is that there are no such good people, and there are no better ingredients. As the Scripture boldly states, there is no one who is righteous, not even one. All people, even the best people, are sinners who have fallen short of the glory of God. Even the best people were conceived with a sin nature. Even our best deeds are as filthy rags in comparison with the perfect goodness, beauty, and holiness of God.[8] If God is going to do anything good through human beings, he will have to do so in spite of compromised ethics, mixed motives, and hypocritical realities.

I have often heard people say that they don't want to become Christians because Christians are hypocrites. They are right in their assessment. It is impossible to be a Christian and *not* be a hypocrite, if by hypocrite we mean someone who lives inconsistently

8. Ps. 14:1–3; Rom. 3:23; Ps. 51:5; Isa. 64:6.

with who they claim to be and what they claim to believe. But our hypocrisy does not negate our Christian faith. Instead, our hypocrisy establishes it. Jesus came not for the righteous but for the unrighteous, not for the sinless but for sinners. There is no way to *be* a Christian without owning these realities about ourselves. This is why when people stand before the congregation to become members of our church, the first question they must answer publicly is, "Do you acknowledge yourself to be a sinner in the sight of God, justly deserving his displeasure, and without hope save in his sovereign mercy?" Only those who answer yes to this question can qualify to become church members.

The second question new members must affirm is, "Do you believe in the Lord Jesus Christ as the Son of God and Savior of sinners, and do you receive and rest upon him alone for salvation as he offered in the gospel?"

Only those who answer yes to both questions understand what it means to be a Christian. We are not saintly people who have earned our place. Rather, we are sinful people who have been saved by grace.

If God worked only with people who are not hypocrites, he would have no one to work with besides Jesus. The question is not whether Christians are hypocrites, because we all most certainly are. Rather, the question is whether we are self-aware and humble in our hypocrisy and rightly saddened by it. God opposes the hypocritical proud, but he gives grace to the hypocritical humble. To self-congratulating moralists who pray, "Thank you, my God, that I am not like other men," he answers with a verdict of judgment. To self-aware sinners who pray, "Have mercy on me, the sinner," he answers with a verdict of justifying grace.[9]

9. James 4:6; Luke 18:9–14.

I believe that there will be three surprises for all of us when we get to heaven. First, we will be surprised to discover that some who were known in this world as good people are not there. Second, we will be surprised that others who were known as bad people are there. And when we've been given the chance to see Jesus face to face in all of his glory, we will be surprised that we are there.

Based on what the Bible teaches about salvation—that it is by grace alone, through faith alone, and in Christ alone—I believe with all of my heart that heaven will be populated with many people whom we knew as saints. These are the people who, in this life, became visibly and increasingly Christlike as faithful bearers of the Spirit's fruit of love, joy, peace, patience, kindness, goodness, gentleness, faithfulness, and self-control.[10] These are also the people who, though being visibly virtuous and holy and good in this life, put their trust not in these things but rather in the life, death, burial, and resurrection of Christ as their only hope in life and in death.

In heaven, there will also be people who were not as visibly virtuous and holy and good in this life, but who nonetheless were received into God's kingdom on the same basis as those who were: by grace, through faith, in Christ. Though these words from a recovering alcoholic priest will sound scandalous to some, they are nonetheless true:

> Among the countless number of people standing in front of the throne and Lamb, dressed in white robes . . . I shall see the prostitute who tearfully told me she could find no other employment to support her two-year-old son. I shall see the

---

10. Gal. 5:22–23.

woman who had an abortion and is haunted by guilt and remorse . . . the businessman besieged with debt who sold his integrity in a series of desperate transactions; the insecure clergyman [ahem . . .] addicted to being liked, who never challenged his people from the pulpit and longed for unconditional love; the sexually abused teen molested by his father and now selling his body on the street . . . There they are. There *we* are—the multitude who so wanted to be faithful, who at times got defeated, soiled by life, and bested by trials, wearing the bloodied garments of life's tribulations, but through it all clung to faith.[11]

A broken hallelujah is still a hallelujah. In the ears of God, it is a sweet sound.

Through Jesus, the God who is holy, who lives in unapproachable light, and whose eyes are too pure to look upon evil *welcomes* sinners and eats with them, even as he tends gently to their weary cries for mercy.[12] And as he welcomes them, he also empowers them to participate in his work.

❦

I have always loved banana bread. I am still unsure why they call it bread because in taste, texture, and calories, it's more like a cake. Banana bread is not only a snack or dessert but also a metaphor for what God can do with questionable ingredients. As most bakers know, the key ingredient in banana bread is the rotten

---

11. Brennan Manning, *The Ragamuffin Gospel* (Colorado Springs: Multnomah, 2008), Kindle.
12. 1 Tim. 6:16; Hab. 1:13; Luke 15:1–2.

banana. Not ripe but rotten. Not yellow but brown. Not firm but mushy. Not smooth but slimy. Brown, mushy, slimy, and rotten *must* go into the mixing bowl if the banana bread is going to be what it is meant to be. When all that is brown, mushy, slimy, and rotten is mixed and warmed with sweeter, more savory ingredients such as sugar, salt, butter, and flour, it eventually comes out as a melt-in-your-mouth masterpiece.

God creates a similar kind of goodness from the ingredient of sinners who have become self-aware, humble, and contrite regarding their rotten realities. This includes sinners like the once adulterous, murderous David who prayed, "Have mercy on me, O God, according to your steadfast love; according to your abundant mercy blot out my transgressions. Wash me thoroughly from my iniquity, and cleanse me from my sin!" Famously, the heading to this prayer is addressed to the director of music as a psalm of David when Nathan the prophet confronted David about his adulterous abuse of Bathsheba. At the time of their sexual encounter, Bathsheba was married to one of David's most loyal friends and soldiers, Uriah the Hittite, whom David subsequently murdered after discovering that Bathsheba was pregnant with his child. Centuries later, the gospel of Matthew mentions David's "slimy rotten" predatorial, power-abusing, libido-ingratiating sin in the family tree of Jesus, where we read, "Jesse [was] the father of David the king. And David was the father of Solomon *by the wife of Uriah.*"[13]

This same David wrote nearly half of the psalms. He is the one about whom God later said, "I have found in David the son of Jesse a man after my heart, who will do all my will."[14] Most

---

13. Ps. 51:1–2; Matt. 1:6, emphasis mine.
14. Acts 13:22.

notably, he is also the one that the New Testament writers had in mind when they repeatedly called Jesus "the Son of David."

One time at a wedding reception, I met a woman named Lindsey. She told me that she liked my homily and wished she could worship at our church. I told her that our doors are always open to her, to which she replied, "Oh no, pastor. You don't understand. I'm too big of a sinner to fit in at any church." I explained to her that according to Jesus, it's impossible to be too much of a sinner for church, because the church is *for* sinners and sinners only. The only people who should feel out of place at church are those who aren't sinful enough. Church has nothing to offer to those who don't believe themselves to be sinners. The same is true of Jesus.

If you have ever doubted Jesus' love and affection for you, are you willing to reconsider? Will you start by moving just one inch closer to him and see what happens? Sometimes if you give Jesus one inch of your trust, he will respond by giving you a hundred miles of love and affection. Sometimes if you give Jesus one thimbleful of pleading, he will return to you an ocean full of compassion and care. Also, if you ever find yourself wishing that you could know Jesus more, that you could walk more closely with him, and that you could receive his mercies anew, do you realize that the very fact that you wish for these things is a sign that his favor is already upon you? Any desire that is in you to know him, no matter how small, is evidence of his immeasurable desire to have and to hold you. Any nudging you may feel to be close to him, no matter how timid, is a sign that he has taken a leap in your direction. He leaped all the way from heaven to earth to be with you.

Poor, wretched sinner, don't ever think that you are too poor or too wretched to belong in church or to Jesus. Where your sin abounds, his grace always superabounds.[15] Once we see this, we'll also see God bearing meaningful fruit through us.

As pastor Rick Warren has said, "In God's garden of grace, even broken trees bear fruit."[16]

There is no more significant garden of God's grace than the garden at Gethsemane. It was in Gethsemane that Jesus pleaded with his Father to spare him of the cup of suffering he was about to bear on the cross for the forgiveness of sins committed by the likes of the nation of Israel, Abraham, Isaac, Jacob, David, and us. There, the Bridegroom prayed, "My Father, if it be possible, let this cup pass from me; nevertheless, not as I will, but as you will."[17]

As we now know in retrospect, it was the Father's will to crush his only begotten Son, so that he would never have any need to crush us: "It was the will of the LORD to crush him; he has put him to grief; when his soul makes an offering for guilt, he shall see his offspring . . . the will of the LORD shall prosper in his hand. Out of the anguish of his soul he shall see and be satisfied . . . [making] many to be accounted righteous, and he shall bear their iniquities."[18]

Jesus, the Son of David, willingly became the Suffering Servant so that David and all who are like him might not only be spared but be turned into a sweet offering of his grace to a weary, hungry world. This was, and this remains, the chief end of a covenant that was made before time began between God

---

15. Rom. 5:20.

16. Rick Warren, "Think about this today: In God's garden of grace . . ." Facebook, October 23, 2015, www.facebook.com/pastorrickwarren/posts/10153653746555903:0.

17. Matt. 26:39.

18. Isa. 53:10–11.

the Father and God the Son. The prophet Ezekiel describes it as God's "covenant of peace," which is an everlasting covenant that, like God's vows of betrothal and marriage to his sometimes-straying people, can never be reversed or undone.

The language of covenant may sound old-fashioned, but the dialog between the Father and the Son captures powerfully the nature—and profound cost—of the covenant of peace. The covenant is pictured honorably, beautifully, and compellingly by Puritan pastor and writer John Flavel:

> Father: My Son, here is a company of poor miserable souls, that have utterly undone themselves, and now lie open to my justice. Justice demands satisfaction for them or will satisfy itself in the eternal ruin of them. What shall be done for these souls?
>
> Son: Oh my Father, such is my love and pity for them that, rather than they shall perish eternally, I will be responsible for them as their Surety. Bring in all thy bills, that I may see what they owe thee. Lord, bring them all in, that there may be no after-reckonings with them. At my hand thou shalt require it. I will rather choose to suffer thy wrath than they should suffer it. Upon me, Father, upon me be all their debt.
>
> Father: But my Son, if thou undertake for them, thou must reckon to pay the last cent. Expect no discounts. If I spare them, I will not spare thee.
>
> Son: Content, Father. Let it be so. Charge it all to me. I am able to pay it. And though it prove a kind of undoing to me, though it impoverish all my riches, empty all my treasures, yet I am content to undertake it.[19]

---

19. John Flavel, *The Whole Works of the Rev. Mr. John Flavel* (London: W. Baynes and Son, 1820), I:61.

It turns out that the reason God can set the bar so low for us is that he set it so high for Jesus, who cleared the bar on our behalf. Now every rotten, decimated, or even dead thing in our lives can be made alive again. Everything in us that has been lost can be found again. Every place in us that has been starved for food, family, and love can be filled again. The Father watches and waits for his prodigals to return Home.

Knowing this to be true, how can we delay for another moment?

How can we keep ourselves from singing?

PROLOGUE 8

THE CHURCH BASEMENT

I say we start bringing church basement dynamics back into church sanctuaries.

The church basement is where addiction recovery groups often meet. It's where lives are transformed, as strugglers get honest and back on their feet.

Maybe recovery groups prefer the basement because the air is cooler down there. Or maybe it's because hitting bottom and losing everything that's dear to you brings you to the lowest places. Hitting bottom, if we survive it, awakens us to the fact that we never grow past our need for healing. Admitting we are frail and incomplete is not a sign of weakness but a sign of strength. It's what makes the healing possible. The bleeding woman who got on the ground to touch the hem of Jesus' garment found this to be true. Jacob, who wrestled on the ground with God all night long, also found this to be true.

As with the woman, the bleeding stops for addicts in the low place.

As with Jacob, the ability to limp back into the world with humble, sober strength starts with wrestling on the ground.

We know we have come to the basement when our fingers stop pointing outward and start pointing inward. We know we have come to the low place of healing when we stop shifting blame and start confessing. "Confess your sins to one another . . . that you may be healed."[1]

---

1. James 5:16.

Full confession goes public. When you stand up to speak in a recovery group, the first thing you do is tell people your name. After that, you state your biggest problem, which is the one you see in the mirror. You admit you are in the ditch you are in not because of external influences or politicians or other people but because of you. You are in recovery not because you are somebody else's victim but because you have become your own worst nightmare, a hazard to yourself, drowning in a sea of porn, prostitutes, booze, narcotics, food, work, narcissism, or toxic religion.

Excuses are not permitted in recovery groups. No more finger-pointing or shifting blame. No more playing the victim. It's just you, standing exposed in front of the group and declaring, "Hi. I'm so-and-so, and I am [insert addiction]." In solidarity and empathy, the room responds, "Hello, so-and-so," which is just another way of saying, "Us too." Then you start telling your story, in which you admit powerlessness over your addiction and your inability to manage it, lament the injury that you have inflicted on others, and declare your belief that only a "power greater than ourselves" in the context of safe, accountable community can restore you to sanity, save you from the mess you have created for yourself, and help you make amends with injured parties.

Admitting self-defeat is key to successful recovery. It involves raw honesty about your worst qualities and the destructive decisions you have made. It requires you to make amends with those who have suffered because of your choices. Recovery is built on the foundation of embracing weakness and your lack of control, which is the first essential step to getting well. God opposes the proud but gives grace to the humble.[2] When you are weak, then—and only then—can you become strong.[3]

Recovery groups sometimes get criticized for being too vague about the so-called higher power who helps addicts get off the ground. Instead of calling on God or Jesus, participants are often invited to call on "god as you understand him." The critiques are warranted because a god of our own making is no god at all. As atheist philosopher Voltaire is quoted as saying, "In the beginning God created man in his own image, and man has been trying to repay the favor ever since."

Any god who gets reduced to our imaginations and sensibilities and preferences is, in truth, more of an invented personal assistant or consultant than a god. Inventing a god of our own making keeps us in control, which contradicts the admission that we are out of control. It also negates and undermines the godness of God. For God to be known truly, he must reveal himself to us, not be created or recreated by us. He must do all the censoring, revising, and correcting to align us to himself. We are unwise when we attempt to relate to him in the reverse.

For others in recovery, *God* and *Jesus* do make their way to the center of higher-power vocabulary, belief, and practice. In fact, the Twelve-Step program has its origins in Christianity and has served as a tool to lead many women and men to Christ. So if the foundation of the program is indeed Christian, why not start with God and Jesus *as* the higher power? Why give participants a choice? While I might not always understand, several years ago I found out one reason why recovery groups adopt a more general approach.

---

2. James 4:6.
3. 2 Cor. 12:10.

I first met Samantha and Greg through a mutual friend who recommended that they come to me for pastoral counseling. They were both recovering alcoholics who had been together for a few months, and they were seeking advice because Samantha had become pregnant unexpectedly. Greg had recently gotten divorced from another woman, they had no money, and they needed help making decisions about what was next for them and their unborn child. Samantha had also been experiencing anxiety and panic attacks. Our friend told Samantha and Greg that she thought I could help them and that as a pastor I could do so free of charge.

In our first meeting, Samantha shared her reservations about receiving counsel from a Christian pastor. Pointedly, she asked me to refrain from bringing Jesus into our conversations. "If you mention the name Jesus," she said, "you will probably never see me again. Every person who has ever talked to me about Jesus has done more scolding than encouraging and more condemning than loving. I am done with Jesus talk. Will you respect that?"

I told Samantha and Greg that some people, believing themselves to be faithful, offer warped and judgmental pictures of Jesus. The Jesus Samantha described to me was a Jesus with whom I, too, could not relate. The true Jesus—the one we are introduced to in the Bible—is not a Jesus who scolds, shames, and condemns people in Samantha and Greg's predicament. He is the opposite of that. He has a tender spot in his heart for those who've been caught in their predicament. He will not move away from them in a posture of rejection and scorn but wishes to move toward them in a posture of gentleness and care. He welcomes sinners and eats with them, and he loves to prepare banquets for prodigals who come limping home.[4] He is *not* prone to scold, shame, and condemn. Isn't this great news?

"So will you avoid saying his name, or not?" Samantha replied.

As a Christian pastor, I was pressed to decide. Would I dig in my heels? Would I assert that if they want free counseling, then they must accept Jesus and me as a package deal? Or would I meet Samantha and Greg where they were and see where He Who Must Not Be Named might take the conversation?

Paul's encounter with the intellectuals of Athens, Greece, came to mind, whose initial belief in a higher power was more vague than it was specific. Instead of scolding, shaming, or condemning them, Paul began the conversation with an affirmation of their belief in a higher power. "Men of Athens, I see that you are very religious." Starting from that place, Paul led them on a journey of history and logic that revealed Jesus *as* the true God whom they sought to know. A conversation that began with "god as you understand him" would end with "now you see that this god is actually Jesus." Several of the Athenian Greeks believed.[5]

So I agreed to Samantha's conditions and we had several rich, mutually encouraging conversations in which Jesus was never mentioned, but his vision for flourishing was woven throughout. To my humble surprise, I learned more about God from the expressed longings of these two agnostic addicts than I have from many Christian commentaries and preachers. They also learned some things from me.

---

4. Luke 15:1–32.
5. Acts 17:16–34.

Toward the end of our season of counseling, both Samantha and Greg declared a newfound love for and belief in Jesus. I officiated their wedding in her parents' living room when she was nearly eight months pregnant. Samantha later became a deaconess in our church. She and Greg started inviting their friends from Alcoholics Anonymous to church, where many of them also shifted from a "god as you understand him" higher power mindset to "Jesus is God." Like Samantha and Greg, many of these women and men also became some of the most refreshingly honest, life-giving members of our church community.

Without realizing they were doing so, a group of recovering addicts brought church basement realities into the church sanctuary. They spoke openly of their addictions and confessed their need for Jesus. I like to think that it rubbed off on the rest of us, who are also addicts of a different kind.

Back to Samantha's triggered reaction based on prior Jesus experiences. Why *are* we so fearful of things like scolding, shaming, and condemnation? Why would Samantha and so many others feel traumatized by the thought of this kind of Jesus-talk repeating itself? I believe it is partly because of the false pictures we've been given of Jesus by individuals and entire churches that emphasize judgment over grace. I also believe it is because we know deep down that we really do fall short and that we, if left to ourselves, will never be enough. We don't really believe that to err is human, because our hearts tell us we should be perfect—as if the law of God were somehow already written on our hearts.[6]

Our failure to measure up even to our own standards leaves us feeling defensive, ashamed, and prone to medicate and hide. It makes us bristle at things like scolding, shaming, and

6. Rom. 12:12–16; Matt. 5:48.

condemning, while also—and ironically—turning us into people who scold, shame, and condemn. It triggers us to act like Adam and Eve in the garden after they realized that they were naked and felt ashamed. Aware of their own brokenness, they turned against each other and questioned the goodness of God. As it has been said, "hurting people hurt people."

☙❧

I cannot speak for you, but I will for myself. Even though I have prayed and read the Bible almost daily for more than thirty years and preached Jesus weekly for more than twenty-five, I am still not the man I am supposed to be. I am far from being that man. I am also frightened to verbalize the many reasons why. But because I was the one who brought up the honest vulnerability of the church basement, I will give it a try.

Some people wrongly assume that pastors have licked the sin problem, or at least that we have tackled it better than others. In their minds, we are "masters of divinity" who live on a higher plane of spirituality than others. But if you asked our families, our closest friends, and our ministry colleagues, you would discover that we are, in truth, more unlike Jesus than we are like Jesus. The gap between God's perfect purity and our tarnished sinfulness is too great to measure, too insurmountable to overcome, too daunting to dwell upon. "Wretched man that I am! Who will deliver me from this body of death?"[7]

Aleksandr Solzhenitsyn said that "the line separating good and evil passes not through states, nor between classes, nor between political parties either—but right through every human

---

7. Rom. 7:24.

heart . . . Even in the best of all hearts, there remains . . . an uprooted small corner of evil."[8] In my honest moments this not only sounds right, it also feels right. This feeling is there not in spite of but because of the fact that I am a Christian pastor. When your line of work requires an intimate relationship with the Bible—in the same way that an addict's recovery requires an intimate relationship with *The Big Book* of Alcoholics Anonymous—it has a way of humbling you.

Like anyone else, we pastors believe and we doubt. We listen patiently and we lose our tempers, we give selflessly and we act selfishly, we preach and we gossip, we pray and we sometimes cuss. We can be kind and hurtful, hopeful and cynical, tender and abrasive, loving and hateful, courageous and cowardly, faithful and frail, hardworking and lazy. Even at our best, we are a duplicitous bunch. As one pastor remarked to his sharpest critics, "Thank you for saying *only* that about me. Let me tell you, you don't know the half of it."

I am still haunted by the memory of things I did in high school. I wish I could take it all back. Picking up from where I left off in prologue 1, there is one painfully specific memory that I have never been able to shake off. I was insecure, afraid, and trying not to get eaten alive in a world of teenage sharks and minnows. So one day I decided to join the sharks by becoming a class clown. In first period, I shouted across the room to a kind, shy girl named Amy, "You are as ugly as s***!" My words made the whole class laugh, but they made Amy cry. In fourth period that same day, a boy named David gave an incorrect answer to a math problem. I shouted across the room, "You, fool! The answer

---

8. Aleksandr Solzhenitsyn, *The Gulag Archipelago* (New York: Harper Perennial Reissue, 2020), Kindle.

is . . ." I got the answer correct. The class laughed out loud again. And David's spirit was crushed.

I have never felt more ashamed than I did when I made the whole class laugh.

Why do we bully others? Is it not because we are terrified ourselves of being crushed? Why do we act so big toward our frail and imperfect human peers? Is it not because on the inside, we feel invisibly small? Is it not because we aren't familiar with the healing powers of the church basement? Or is it because of something else?

Even as I succeeded in getting the laughs I craved at the expense of a girl who was *not* ugly and a boy who was *not* a fool, I felt like a sick failure for the ugly, foolish things I had done. That sick feeling has never left me. What's more, I imagine that under certain circumstances or pressures, I might still crush other spirits by turning my skilled tongue into a merciless and murderous dagger. Sticks and stones may break your bones, but my words can crush you deeply. I am a man of unclean lips, and I live among a people of unclean lips.

⸙

Three years ago, I unexpectedly ran into an old friend at a Christian conference in my hometown of Nashville. In college, we had participated in juvenile and sometimes dangerous behavior involving alcohol and basically making fools of ourselves. At the time, we thought of ourselves as funny and the life of any party. We often egged each other on in these behaviors. Now here we both were, some thirty years later, all sobered up and participating in a Christian conference. My friend broke the initial, awkward silence and said, "I have only two words for you: I'm so sorry."

"That's three words," I responded.

Then I said, "I'm sorry too. I would also like to introduce you to a better version of the friend you had in college. I am a friend of Jesus now, which I trust will make me a better (and more sober) friend to you." The next morning, my friend showed up unexpectedly at our church, where I was able to serve communion to him and his family. It was full-circle wonderful to be able to do so.

Why do I tell you these sorts of things about myself? Because I think everybody needs to know that pastors and addicts are more alike than we are different. In fact, many pastors are addicts and many addicts are pastors, the awareness of which is what makes us better, not worse, at what we do. Our addictions can range from personal ambition to being in control to having other people's approval, and everything in between. We, too, have a sin problem that will persist until the day we die. We, too, can be our own worst enemies. No amount of effort, positive thinking, or determination will make it otherwise. Admitting this about ourselves—like Isaiah did with his unclean lips, David did with his adultery, and Paul did with his coveting[9]—is not only courageous but healthy. Coming clean improves our relationship with God, the people we are called to serve, and ourselves. Church basement honesty is much more empowering and fruitful than relying on false, wishful verdicts about ourselves as we nudge God out of the picture.

Self-esteem is overrated. Only an esteem that comes from beyond us—from the forgiveness, acquittal, and favor achieved

9. Isa. 6:1–8; Ps. 51; Rom. 7:7–25.

for us on the cross—will be able to help, hold, and sustain us. Jesus' gruesome, haunted exterior resembled our gruesome, haunted interior. The doctrines of grace will become amazing grace only when our cry becomes, "Nothing in my hands I bring; simply to Thy cross I cling. Naked, I come to Thee for dress; helpless, I look to Thee for grace. Foul, I to the fountain fly. Wash me, Savior, or I die."[10]

We can make that cry in confidence because we have a promise in the Bible about what happens if we do: "If we confess our sins, [God] is faithful and just to forgive us our sins and to cleanse us from all unrighteousness."[11]

Rejoice. You are a train wreck.

You are also more loved than you ever dreamed.

---

10. Augustus Toplady, "Rock of Ages" (public domain, 1763).
11. 1 John 1:9.

GOD HAS
BAD TASTE

Y*ou are a train wreck.*

How does that land with you? How does it make you feel?

Some people believe that words like sin, guilt, judgment, wrath, and confession don't belong in the human vocabulary anymore. Such words seem regressive, arcane, primitive, unsophisticated, unenlightened. Too negative, morose, depressing, defeating.

But are they?

Some believe that their inner goodness is a better source of esteem than a love that comes from outside them. Some believe, despite evidence to the contrary, that most people are inherently good. Some believe that the biggest problems in the world are other people and broken systems (where indeed, problems do exist) but take no issue with themselves. Some believe that time spent in the church basement is wasted time. Some believe that Jesus is a thoughtful, inspiring moral teacher, but not a Savior we need to save us from ourselves.

If you don't see Jesus as necessary or yourself as a sinner in need, I invite you to humbly consider Jesus' Sermon on the Mount. This sermon is celebrated by believers and nonbelievers alike as the epicenter of his moral teaching. "I like to live my life by the Sermon on the Mount," we blithely say. But if we think of Jesus only or even chiefly as an inspiring moral teacher and the Sermon on the Mount as our guide, we are either delusional or have not actually read the sermon. Left to ourselves, there is no earthly way we can abide this moral teaching. Here are a few of its disorienting excerpts:

- "You have heard that it was said to those of old, 'You shall not murder . . .' But I say to you that everyone who is angry with his brother will be liable to judgment."[1]
- "You have heard that it was said, 'You shall not commit adultery.' But I say to you that everyone who looks at a woman with lustful intent has already committed adultery with her in his heart."[2]
- "Love your enemies and pray for those who persecute you."[3]
- "No one can serve two masters . . . You cannot serve God and money."[4]
- "Do not be anxious about your life."[5]
- "Judge not, that you be not judged."[6]
- "Whatever you wish that others would do to you, do also to them."[7]
- "Not everyone who says to me, 'Lord, Lord,' will enter the kingdom of heaven . . . Many will say to me, 'Lord, Lord, did we not . . . do many mighty works in your name?' And then will I declare to them, 'I never knew you; depart from me.'"[8]
- "Be perfect, as your heavenly Father is perfect."[9]

---

1. Matt. 5:21–22.
2. Matt. 5:27–28.
3. Matt. 5:44.
4. Matt. 6:24.
5. Matt. 6:25.
6. Matt. 7:1.
7. Matt. 7:12.
8. Matt. 7:21–23.
9. Matt. 5:48.

What is your honest response to these excerpts and others like them? To the teacher who spoke them? One common response is to be perplexed. Jesus is paradoxically kind toward sinners, but also severe toward sin; a forgiving advocate, but also a righteous judge; a tender lamb, but also a roaring lion.[10] Being all of these things at once, he throws us out of whack.

In the Sermon on the Mount and all Scripture, we see a picture of both grace and truth, both love and law. The grace and love of Jesus confirm that he is invitingly approachable. The truth and law of Jesus confirm that he can also be transcendent and dangerous. There is good reason to fear and tremble at the Lord's teaching about morality, ethics, and virtue. But with him there is also forgiveness that he may be feared.[11]

Forgiveness that he may be feared.

There is mystery in this strange connection presented to us in the psalms. But if we can receive it, our fear of God can make it such that we never need be afraid of anything else, including God.

"Fear not, for I am with you; be not dismayed, for I am your God; I will strengthen you, I will help you, I will uphold you with my righteous right hand."[12]

Such a promise provides the kind of safety, shelter, and hope that addicts discover in church basements. It invites us to speak honestly about the things we are most ashamed of and the guilt, hurts, and fears that weary us the most.

But will we believe the promise enough to speak more honestly about ourselves?

---

10. Rom. 11:22.
11. Ps. 130:4.
12. Isa. 41:10.

In 1995, *Newsweek* published an essay called "What Ever Happened to Sin?"[13] As I read the decades-old piece, it struck me how current it still is. The writer, Kenneth Woodward, starts by talking about the history of sin, beginning with Adam and Eve, who, submerged in guilt and fear, resorted to cover-up and blame-shifting strategies to ease themselves.

According to Woodward, accounts like Adam and Eve's have gone out of style. "Who identifies with Adam and Eve these days?" he writes. "Although many people occasionally experience shame—loss of face—guilt requires much more: a recognition of sin and the need to change one's life. Ninety percent of Americans say they believe in God. Yet the urgent sense of personal sin has all but disappeared in the current upbeat style in American religion."

Woodward notes how the monthly Roman Catholic ritual of confessing to a priest has all but disappeared, with only 40 percent of Catholics confessing their sins at a rate of just twice per year. The historic practice of confessing sin together is also downplayed in many Protestant worship services. American Protestants now favor more uplifting, nonconfrontational liturgies, songs, and sermons. A preacher's presumed task is to affirm people's virtue, not to confront people's sin. It often seems to me that for some, the greatest sin a preacher can commit is not to diminish Scripture but to disrupt people's comfort and self-esteem. Any talk about the wrongs and ills within *us* has shifted focus to the

---

13. Kenneth Woodward, "What Ever Happened to Sin?" *Newsweek*, February 5, 1995, www.newsweek.com/what-ever-happened-sin-185180.

wrongs and ills "out there" in broken systems, "those people," and even Scripture itself. According to Woodward, gone are the days when clergy spoke directly to matters that are closer to home, like divorce, pride, greed, and overweening ambition.

Perhaps surprisingly, Woodward does not celebrate the disappearance of sin and guilt from the American lexicon. Instead, he concludes that the most "disabled" among us are the ones who lack self-awareness and experience no guilt. At least those who admit their guilt know there is a better version of themselves to wish for and become.

Woodward's observation in 1995 about the disappearance of sin and guilt continues to be supported by current trends, such as the increasing elimination of biblical themes like sin, guilt, judgment, and wrath from the songs we sing. Such themes are supplanted with new words aimed at keeping positivity and self-esteem intact. For example, one music awards show featured an artist singing John Newton's famous hymn "Amazing Grace." But when she got to the part that says "that saved a wretch like me," she altered the last words to say "that saved *someone* like me." Yet Newton—who wrote the hymn in part as a confession of guilt and contrition based on his former life as a slave trader—purposefully emphasized the reality of his wretchedness. His choice of words was intentional.

When sin ceases to be wretched, grace ceases to be amazing.

And when grace ceases to be amazing, things like grace, forgiveness, and then subsequent truth, beauty, holiness, and virtue cease to move us. When this happens, we become stuck in an insurmountable rut.

I'm going to show my hand here. I have an agenda to win you over to a robust belief in sin and guilt—not chiefly the sin and guilt that are "out there" in other people and the system but the sin and guilt that reside in your heart. I also hope to convince you that owning your sin, weakness, and not-enough-ness is a far better, far more hopeful solution to your emotional fragility than depending on self-esteem, which is based on the mistaken idea that people are essentially good. Across time, place, and culture, we can't even agree on what constitutes good. And, according to Scripture and human experience, all people—including you and me at our very best—are not essentially good. There is something deeply wrong with us. Because of this, our esteem can be derived not from a sense of our own goodness but from belief in the goodness of God.

༄ ~ ༄

In a world where the refrain "most people are good" is often given veto power over the biblical teaching that "no one does good, not even one,"[14] it is important to see how and why the Bible takes such a grim view of our human condition.

Holding nothing back, the prophet Moses observed that "the wickedness of man was great in the earth, and . . . every intention of the thoughts of his heart was only evil continually."[15] Moses is suggesting that if we opened our mouths and said "ahhh," what would be revealed is spiritual sickness instead of spiritual health, rotten compost instead of ripened fruit, moral filth instead of moral virtue, the stench of death instead of the aroma of life.

"Their throat is an open grave," the apostle Paul says. "There is no fear of God before their eyes."[16] Isaiah also says, "We have

---

14. Rom. 3:12.
15. Gen. 6:5.
16. Rom. 3:13–18.

all become like one who is unclean, and all our righteous deeds are like a polluted garment."[17]

It is not just our worst deeds but even our righteous deeds that are problematic in God's sight. If Isaiah had been born much later, one might wonder whether he had been reading the philosopher Friedrich Nietzsche, who argued that even our best deeds have self-centered motives behind them. According to Nietzsche, we do good not for the sake of the good itself but rather for the sake of being noticed and applauded and of gaining more power. Our best virtues, Nietzsche said, are less about serving others and more about securing a reward for ourselves. It's a cynical view, to be sure, but it is also hard to argue against. As one theologian is similarly quoted as saying, "The main thing between you and God is not so much your sins; it's your damnable good works."[18]

As a faithful minister and writer of one-third of the New Testament who recognized these things in himself, the apostle Paul includes himself among the walking dead: "For I know that nothing good dwells *in me*, that is, in my flesh. For I have the desire to do what is right, but not the ability to carry it out. For I do not do the good I want, but the evil I do not want is what I keep on doing . . . when I want to do right, evil lies close at hand . . . Wretched man that I am! Who will deliver me from this body of death?"[19] Here we see Paul offer a confession similar to Isaiah's cry that he was a man of unclean lips.

Moses, Paul, and Isaiah. Three notable servants of God, each among the most faithful and fruitful of his time, grieving the helplessly corrupt human condition and the way it has rendered

---

17. Isa. 64:6.
18. I have often heard this quote attributed to John Gerstner by his former students.
19. Rom. 7:18–24, emphasis mine.

even them feeble and frail—cracked about the head along with the rest of us, and sadly in need of mending. There is none who does good, not even one. We are a people of unclean lips.

The sequence of Paul's self-appraisal in his New Testament letters drills the point down even deeper. In an early letter he calls himself "Paul, an apostle," then later "the least of the apostles," then later "the very least of all the saints." Finally, as he nears the end of his ministry and the peak of his moral virtue, he insists in a letter to the young minister Timothy that "Christ Jesus came into the world to save sinners, of whom I am the foremost."[20] Even as he grew into the best version of himself, Paul kept in touch with his need for an esteem that came from outside himself.

I can relate to Paul in this. Some days, I feel less holy and virtuous than I did when I first believed in Christ. Some days, I feel more fraudulent in my faith than authentic, more disingenuous than real, more bent than straight, and—concerning my call to ministry—more unqualified than qualified. It's a trustworthy saying that deserves full acceptance: Christ Jesus came into the world to save sinners, of whom I am the foremost. Sorry, Paul. You'll have to take first place in something else now.

More than three decades as a follower of Christ and I actually *do* feel this way much of the time. Do you?

Like Paul, the more mature we become *in* Christ, the deeper we will feel our need *for* Christ. The stronger our faith in Christ becomes, the weaker in ourselves we will feel. "The feel of faith is not strength but dependent weakness."[21] This weakness that we feel in ourselves is meant not to discourage but to encourage. Who are the happiest in God's kingdom? It is not those who feel

---

20. Gal. 1:1; 1 Cor. 15:9; Eph. 3:8; 1 Tim. 1:15.
21. This quote has been attributed to Rev. Joe Novenson.

strong, put together, and sufficient in themselves, but those who are poor in spirit, who mourn, who are meek, and who hunger and thirst for a righteousness that only Jesus can supply.[22]

Add to Moses, Isaiah, and Paul the great King David and famed "man after God's own heart,"[23] who also authored half of the psalms. In one of those psalms, he begged God for mercy in light of *his* self-appraisal, saying, "According to your great compassion blot out my transgressions. Wash away all my iniquity and cleanse me from my sin . . . Surely I was sinful at birth, sinful from the time my mother conceived me . . . Cleanse me . . . Wash me . . . Hide your face from my sins and blot out all my iniquity . . . Create in me a pure heart . . . grant me a willing spirit."[24]

Even Jesus' family tree included the wretched, including two men who offered their wives to predators, a deceiver, a prostitute, an incest victim, an abuser of power, a neglectful father, a womanizer, a coward, and others like them.[25] Many of these unsavory characters are also listed in the so-called faith hall of fame in Hebrews 11:1–39. This includes Abraham, Isaac, Rahab, Solomon, and others. Look them up and read their stories. As you do, consider the very good news that God has bad taste.

Cerⁿⁿ

It is good to be reminded often that God has bad taste. That he welcomes even—no, especially—the wretched into his circle, family, and heart.

The Bible testifies that Christ Jesus came into the world to

22. Matt. 5:1–12.
23. Acts 13:22.
24. Ps. 51:1–12 NIV.
25. Matt. 1:1–17.

save sinners and, in saving sinners, to befriend, adopt, and tend mercifully to them.

Zacchaeus was a perpetrator of systemic theft and injustice. Mary Magdalene was possessed and traumatized by a demon. The woman caught in adultery was caught in adultery. There are many others like them, which leads us to conclude that God reserves special attention and tender loving care for those who know that they miss the mark. Likewise, he takes issue with those who think of themselves as morally superior, popular, shiny, rich, well networked, or intelligent. This is no doubt why morally upright people can be so difficult to reach with the message of Christ while morally flattened people are often easier to reach.

When we survey the list of Jesus' most famous followers, it appears that he searched the church basement to find them. Their ranks include the "morally bankrupt, bottom of the barrel" people. The "stuck in the compost, stick in the mud" people. "Throats like open graves" people. "Groping at the hem of his garment in the dirt on the ground" people. "Violating and impregnating another man's wife" kinds of people.[26] "Caught in the act" kinds of people. The losers, not the winners. Tired prostitutes, not triumphant Pharisees. Those who lack self-esteem, not those who have self-esteem. Those who are tired of trying to be good, not those who insist that they are good. Those who receive Jesus' merciful verdicts, not those who pronounce boastful verdicts over themselves. Those who beat their breasts with broken and contrite hearts, not those who parade their virtue from prideful hearts. Those who humble themselves, not those who exalt themselves.

---

26. Matt. 1:6.

Those who understand that the feel of faith is not strength but dependent weakness.

"Why does your teacher eat with tax collectors and sinners?" the Pharisees asked the tax collector Matthew and his fellow disciples-sinners. Irritated by the question, Jesus interrupted and defended his disciples by declaring, "Those who are well have no need of a physician, but those who are sick. Go and learn what this means: 'I desire mercy, and not sacrifice.' For I came not to call the righteous, but sinners."[27]

On another occasion, Jesus warned some holier-than-thou folk that tax collectors and prostitutes were entering God's kingdom in front of them.[28] How could this be? Why was this so? Because the tax collectors and prostitutes saw what the religious leaders could not, that their biggest problem is not "out there" in broken systems and other people but within their own, broken selves.

"Wretched man that *I* am. Who will rescue *me* from this body of death?"

When we appraise ourselves honestly, the good news that "God has bad taste" and that he welcomes sinners to eat with him will no longer sound offensive to us. Instead, it will become a sweet sound, like the sound of amazing grace. It will also feel good, smell good, and taste good.

Proud moralists watch the clock impatiently during communion.

Weary sinners eat and sip slowly, savoring every bit.

Proud moralists want self-affirming, self-esteem boosting, dishonest liturgies and songs and sermons.

---

27. Matt. 9:9–13.
28. Matt. 21:31.

Weary sinners have no energy left for this kind of fakery. Instead, they receive every truthful word with thanks, especially the ones who declare that God is good and they are not.

Ⓒ⌇⌇⑨

If Moses, Isaiah, David, and Paul could so freely confess sin and guilt, what stops us from doing the same? If Jesus really does have bad taste and he knows the very worst things about us, what stops him from welcoming and eating with us? Answer: nothing.

Let this sink in. Jesus welcomes and receives us not despite the worst things about us but because of them. His favorite thing to do is to undo our self-inflicted regret with his grace, tend to our self-inflicted hurt with his mercy, and quiet our self-inflicted fear with his love. That's who he is, and that is what he does.

Before we can reap the full benefits of what Jesus is and does for us, we must take an honest look in the mirror and "make a searching and fearless inventory of ourselves."[29] When we honestly look at ourselves, we begin to see our need for him. In the awareness of our need and his grace, we can then fearlessly confront ourselves with the question, "What specific evidence is there that I actually need the grace, mercy, and quieting love of Jesus as much as those unsavory people from Bible times did?"

Are you prepared to confront yourself with this question?

Or do you hesitate to place yourself in the company of sinners? If so, why? Is it because you don't see yourself in the adulterous, murderous David? Is it because you don't see in yourself the prostitution of Rahab or the blasphemy and violence of Paul

---

29. Anonymous, *The Big Book of Alcoholics Anonymous* (Twelve Step Study Guides Publishing, 2015), Kindle.

or the deceit of Jacob? Is it because you don't relate to those who are familiar with the moral low ground, thereby excluding other sinners from the community of humans even as you exclude yourself from the community of sinners?[30]

When you receive a message from a friend, family member, or coworker that says, "Can we talk?" or worse, "Must talk soon," how does it make you feel? Do such messages feel more threatening than inviting to you? Like somebody is about to call you out and expose you as a fraud? Where do you think this feeling comes from? When you experience it, is it because you know deep down that there are some things about you that, if exposed or talked about, would make you want to run and hide? Is it because you fear that being known would also lead to being rejected?

Enters the real Jesus—who leads with neither scolding nor shaming nor condemnation but with gentleness, welcome, and grace. He invites you to follow him to the church basement, where there is humility, honesty, safety, and freedom to come out of hiding. It is there that he will make you brave. And when you become brave, you will make it your mission to bring the church basement to the church sanctuary, and from there into the world.

There are basically two prayers that can be prayed regarding sin and guilt. The first is, "God, I thank you that I am not like other men, extortioners, unjust, adulterers, or even like this tax collector. I fast twice a week; I give tithes of all that I get." It's a self-esteem-seeking kind of prayer. The kind that avoids the church basement and seeks a platform instead. The kind that sends us home condemned while feeling proud.[31]

---

30. Miroslav Volf, *Exclusion and Embrace* (Nashville: Abingdon, 2019), Kindle.
31. Luke 18:9–14.

The second is, "Almighty and most merciful Father; we err and stray from your ways like lost sheep. We follow too much the devices and desires of our own hearts. We offend against your holy laws. We leave undone those things which we ought to do; and we do those things which we ought not; And there is no saving health in us. But you, O Lord, have mercy upon us. Spare them, O God, who confess their faults. Restore them that are penitent; According to your promises declared unto mankind in Christ Jesus our Lord. And grant, O most merciful Father, for his sake, that we may hereafter live a godly, righteous, and sober life, to the glory of your holy Name. Amen."[32]

Contrary to the former prayer, this latter is a health-and-sobriety-seeking kind of prayer. The kind that avoids the "Jesus" who scolds, shames, and condemns and instead follows *Jesus* into the church basement. The kind that sends us back into the sanctuary and world having been humbled, known, and loved.

Hello, my name is Scott. I am a sinner. Not a general sinner but a particular one. Not a decent one but a rotten one. There is no such thing as a decent sinner because there is no such thing as a decent sin. And as the *Big Book* and the Good Book both affirm, I cannot and will not get better unless and until I admit to God, to myself, and to other human beings the exact nature of my wrongs.[33]

I am an approval addict. I crave praise and fear criticism, even the constructive kind. Sometimes I enjoy the sound of my own name more than the sound of Jesus' name. I always want others to know the best things about me, but never the worst

---

32. Adapted from *The Services of the Book of Common Prayer* (London: William MacIntosh, 1884), 27.

33. Anonymous, *The Big Book*.

things. This leads me to settle for the fake intimacy found in likes, follows, and fans instead of the vulnerable intimacy of having actual friends.

I am also addicted to anger. I got annoyed this week when someone interrupted the flow of my work. I can be an unloving Pharisee toward people I perceive to be unloving Pharisees. Yesterday, I got road rage. Five minutes ago, I resented the simplicity and ease of another person's life.

I am powerless to change myself apart from a higher power. Left to myself, I am out of control. My higher power is Jesus, whose saving health is more essential to me than oxygen. I am able to know him best in the context of a safe, accountable community.

You too?

If you ever need to talk, you can find me in the church basement, where the honest addicts hang out. For it is there and with them that I'm learning, ever so slowly, to feel most at Home.

VAPOR

If the Bible is a party, then Ecclesiastes is the party pooper.

Ecclesiastes is a unique book with a unique writer. He is mighty and rich. He is an influential king with extraordinary power over other people, as evidenced by his many servants and one thousand wives and concubines. Concerning wealth, he has not just a house but many houses. He has not just a garden but many gardens. And wardrobes. And luxury dining. And the best furniture. He also has a supreme intellect. And fame. And unparalleled success in all that he does. As many would say, he has it all.

He also has misery.

Even though this ancient king is "blessed" with so much abundance and prosperity, he seems more perplexed and sorrowful than any other writer in the Bible. Despite having everything he ever dreamed of—or maybe because of it—this man carries many burdens. To the reader's surprise, he finds it nearly impossible to enjoy all the many things that the rest of us spend our lives wishing that we had. Here are just a few expressions of his anguish:

- *Concerning work and success:* "What does man gain by all the toil at which he toils under the sun? . . . All things are full of weariness . . . I turned about and gave my heart up to despair over all the toil of my labors . . . for apart from [God] who can eat or who can have enjoyment? . . . I have seen slaves on horses, and princes walking on the ground like slaves."[1]

- *Concerning knowledge and wisdom:* "He who increases knowledge increases sorrow."[2]

- *Concerning possessions and pleasure:* "I made great works. I built houses and planted vineyards for myself . . . I had also great possessions . . . I got singers, both men and women, and many concubines . . . I kept my heart from no pleasure . . . and behold, all was vanity and a striving after wind."[3]

- *Concerning money:* "[My] eyes are never satisfied with riches . . . He who loves money will not be satisfied with money . . . a man to whom God gives wealth, possessions, and honor, so that he lacks nothing of all that he desires, yet God does not give him power to enjoy them."[4]

- *Concerning everything:* "All is vanity."[5]

If this powerful, wealthy, famous man were alive today and got caught on video saying these sorts of things, can you imagine the public lashing he would receive? "Poor little rich guy having a pity party," people might say. "Must be hard living in all those mansions, sleeping with all those women, hosting all those parties, eating all those fine meats, counting all that cash. Must be rough with all those people waiting on him hand and foot. Such a hard life. How does he do it? Rich idiot."

Or something like that.

---

1. Eccl. 1:2–3, 8; 2:20, 25; 10:7.
2. Eccl. 1:18.
3. Eccl. 2:4–11.
4. Eccl. 4:8; 5:10; 6:2.
5. Eccl. 12:8.

A few years ago, I was invited to speak at a conference which took place at a luxury resort on the California coast. Nestled in the midst of one of the world's wealthiest neighborhoods, the resort was gorgeous in natural beauty and curated opulence. During a break, my wife and I went for a walk along the coast, where we passed by dozens of multi-million-dollar mansions, each with its own private beachfront area. At one point, I turned to her and said, "Must be rough having to live like this." In her characteristic gentleness and wisdom, she responded, "Yes, you're right, Scott. It is rough for these people. You often tell our church to be kind because every person we meet is fighting a hard battle. That includes people living in opulent California mansions, right?"

In an essay about celebrity life and culture, one New York journalist observed, "I pity celebrities. No, I do . . . When God wants to play a really rotten practical joke on you, he grants you your deepest wish and then giggles merrily when you suddenly realize you want to kill yourself . . . [These celebrities] wanted fame. They worked, they pushed . . . The night each of them became famous they wanted to shriek with relief. Finally! Now they were adored! Invincible! Magic! . . . The morning after the night each of them became famous they wanted to take an overdose of barbiturates. All their fantasies had been realized, yet the reality was still the same. If they were miserable before, they were twice as miserable now . . . The disillusionment turned them howling and insufferable."[6]

The journalist's thesis is supported by a long list of people

6. Cynthia Heimel, "1980–1989: The Celebrity Decade," *Village Voice*, January 2, 1990, accessed February 6, 2020, www.villagevoice.com/2020/02/06/1980-1989-the-celebrity-decade/.

who ascended to fame and fortune, but whose lives ended in misery. No human soul was made to bear the weight of fame except the soul of Jesus. Jesus alone has the character and capacity to stand on a pedestal and not get crushed by it. Only he belongs there, because the chief end of all creation is to glorify and enjoy *him* forever,[7] and his chief end is to receive all the glory and be the object of his creation's joy.

As part of creation, we humans—all of us—are meant to worship versus being worshiped, to stand in awe versus having others stand in awe of us, to bow the knee versus being bowed unto, to exalt Christ's fame and fortune versus seeking our own fame and fortune. Ann Voskamp writes, "Celebrity or saint, scoundrel or steward, there's a plot of dirt waiting for us all just the same. Ashes to ashes, dust to dust, is the way of all of us . . . Don't follow me. Don't follow anybody but the Perfect One who had to take on a body. Don't follow anybody made of flesh, because flesh will fail and fall. Follow Jesus alone, who alone can save."[8]

Consider these names: Novelist Ernest Hemingway. Fashion designers Alexander McQueen and Kate Spade. Painter Mark Rothko. Nirvana frontman Kurt Cobain. Each one, at the peak of fame and fortune, committed suicide. Consider also popular singers Amy Winehouse, Janis Joplin, Elvis Presley, and Jim Morrison and famous actor Heath Ledger. Each one, also at the peak of his or her fame and fortune, died of a drug overdose.

Several years ago, I heard famous singer Mariah Carey give an unexpected answer to a question she received at the peak of

7. Ann Voskamp, "About Celebrities and Living Small: A Lent to Repent and Live in the Universe of Jesus," *annvoskamp.com*, accessed February 1, 2022, www.goodreads .com/author_blog_posts/20978569-about-celebrities-living-small-a-lent-to-repent-live -in-the-univers.
8. Ibid.

her career. Still very young, she was reported to have achieved more number one hits than anyone in the history of music except Elvis Presley and the Beatles. When asked what goals she had left to achieve, her answer was, "Happiness."

Indeed, every person you meet, and every person you wish you could meet, is fighting a hard battle.

This includes rich and famous people. Of course, it also includes those who are destitute financially, relationally, vocationally, or otherwise. It includes the masses who live between the extremes. Thoreau told the truth about us all. "The mass of men lead lives of quiet desperation."[9]

Compassion, anyone?

Nobody who is awake and has lived a few years can deny that life is hard. But what are we to make of people like the writer of Ecclesiastes, or for that matter philosophers such as Camus, Sartre, Nietzsche, Arendt, and others like them who can't seem to stop talking about the darker side of life? Who wants to listen to or sit with people for whom the glass is always half empty? Our mothers and mentors taught us that if we can't say anything nice, then we shouldn't say anything at all. Look on the bright side. Keep on the sunny side of life. Don't worry, be happy. How does the message of Ecclesiastes, inspired by the God who created us and loves us even more than our mothers and mentors do, fit into what they taught us?

Hopefully, our mothers and mentors also taught us that life

---

9. Henry David Thoreau, *Walden; or, Life in the Woods* (New York: Dover, 2012), Kindle.

can be difficult. But if we find ourselves having little patience for the somber tone of Ecclesiastes, if we seem unwilling to look at, think about, or acknowledge the true and expansive pain of things, if we avoid the stories that are more dystopian than happily ever after, if our playlists don't include any songs in a minor key, then we are doing ourselves and the world a disservice. We are also missing out on a precious gift that God has prepared for those who are willing to admit and contend with their own hard battles.

"How are you doing?"

"I'm fine."

No, you're not. Neither am I.

Denying the pain and sorrow that come with being alive is a form of hypocrisy. It is a choice we make to distance ourselves from the truth, or at least part of the truth, and live in a pretentious fairyland instead. When we do this, we cut ourselves off from what we were made for—loving intimacy with God and others. Intimacy cannot happen without honesty. The absence of honesty cuts off our ability to be known. It isolates us, forcing us to be alone even when we are among colleagues, at a party, around a family dinner table, or in a marriage bed. "It is not good . . . [to] be alone."[10] And there is no worse way to be alone than when we feel alone even while sharing space together with others.

Our vulnerability to isolation is one of the many reasons why we need the honesty of Ecclesiastes. With Holy Spirit–inspired, raw truth telling, the writer—let's call him Solomon[11]—grants

---

10. Gen. 2:18.

11. There is debate about who the author of Ecclesiastes is, although some attribute it to Solomon because of how the author portrays himself as a wealthy king, which was also true of Solomon.

us permission to tell the truth about our own sorrows and our own selves. He invites us to come clean as church-basement dwellers do. This is the first and essential step toward becoming whole again. With community comes wholeness. And yet community can happen only when one person tells the truth about life, which leads others to chime in, "Yeah? I get that. Same here."

Every once in a while, we need an Eeyore in our lives who has the courage to say, "This hurts. Living hurts. Everything . . . just . . . hurts." Sometimes friends and loved ones need *us* to be the Eeyore, to go first in giving voice to our sorrows to signal that it's okay for them to give voice to theirs, too.

When the writer of Ecclesiastes says that everything is vanity, the Hebrew word he uses means "vapor." Holding on to the good things in life is about as easy as holding on to a fistful of smoke. No matter how we try to keep its fumes within our grasp, they leak out between our fingers. In the same way, life leaks out of us every day. Like a sandcastle on the beach, everything and everyone dear to us will eventually be swept away. The breath you just took is one more toward your last. This is also true of your most recent kiss, your most recent payday, your most recent nap, your most recent feast, as well as the most recent book, movie, show, song, or time spent walking in the park.

It is all so wonderful.

It is also all so tragically fleeting.

As Melville reflected, "That mortal man who hath more of joy than sorrow in him, that mortal man cannot be true—not true, or undeveloped. With books the same. The truest of all men was the Man of Sorrows, and the truest of all books is

Solomon's . . . Ecclesiastes is the fine hammered steel of woe. 'All is vanity.' ALL."[12] Life is tragic, and then we die. This is the plain, unfiltered truth about the universe and us. None can escape it.

Everything is vapor. Everyone is leaking.

The wages of sin is death.[13]

12. Herman Melville, *Moby Dick* (public domain, 2019), Kindle.
13. Rom. 6:23.

HOMESICK

When we bring our sorrows out of hiding, hope follows closely behind. Admitting and owning the diagnosis, it turns out, is the first step in the direction of healing.

This kind of honesty—the raw kind—does not come naturally to me. From my youngest years, I lived in a world where expressing one's distress was considered bad taste. One of my earliest memories is when I was told that it is unacceptable to complain, yell, or cry. In twenty-six years of marriage, my wife and daughters have seen me cry only a handful of times. Early on, it must have been drummed into my mind that to "whine like a little baby" or "cry like a girl" instead of acting like I've got it all together is unacceptable. I never understood what was wrong with babies and girls. Jesus was especially fond of babies. Adam came most alive when God gave him a "she" to share life with.

Despite this upbringing, my personality type lends itself to honest speech, especially the kind that spotlights how agitating, disturbing, and wearying things can be in this fallen world of ours. I suspect that sometimes, this attribute of mine can wear other people out. One group of experts describes my personality type as follows: "[They] are self-aware, sensitive, and reserved. They are emotionally honest, creative, and personal, but can also be moody and self-conscious. Withholding themselves from others due to feeling vulnerable and defective . . . they typically have problems with melancholy, self-indulgence, and self-pity."[1]

---

1. The Enneagram Institute, "The Individualist: Enneagram Type Four," *enneagram institute.com*, www.enneagraminstitute.com/type-4.

That's me. Want to be friends?

If I were a betting man, I would bet that the writer of Ecclesiastes and I share the same personality type. Most days I would rather be more naturally upbeat and quick to see the sunny side of life. But I guess it's best to accept and learn to love the person God has made me to be. As Steve Jobs said in a commencement speech at Stanford, our time is limited, so we shouldn't waste it living somebody else's life by letting "the noise of others' opinions drown out [our] own inner voice."[2]

Knowing that my own "inner voice" bears similarity to the voice of Eeyore, I have always secretly wished that I *could* live somebody else's life. For most of my life, I haven't wanted to be so tuned in to the dark side of things. I just am.

In social gatherings, I often get this feeling that I am the most annoying person in the room. For some reason I can't quite explain, I feel like a fish out of water. Like the odd one out. The ugly duckling. The impostor who doesn't belong.

I have never been told that I am annoying at a social gathering, but I have felt annoying—and with it, annoyed toward myself. Why can't I just savor the moment? Why can't I enter in more easily than I do to the laughter and feasting and levity? Why do thoughts come into my head like, "This is fun for now, but like everything, it isn't going to last." Why aren't I funnier than I am? Why aren't I more lighthearted, easygoing, and pleasant? Why can't I be more fully present, more in the moment, more engaged? Why can't I be more likable? Why can't I be more like *other* people?

A couple of years ago at a dinner gathering where I was feeling sad but hiding behind a smile, I was part of a conversation

---

2. Steve Jobs, "'You've Got to Find What You Love,' Jobs Says," *Stanford.edu*, Stanford University, June 14, 2005, https://news.stanford.edu/2005/06/14/jobs-061505/.

that helped me think better about being me. There were four of us in the conversation, and three of us began teasing the fourth about I can't remember what. What I do remember is how she responded to the teasing. Jovially and in good fun, she stopped the conversation and said to the three of us, "Let's just get something straight here. I don't like me either. That's right. Even *I* don't like me!" We all laughed at our friend's remark in response to our teasing. Then I thought quietly to myself, "You too?"

I don't actually dislike myself. It is more accurate to say that I don't always feel at home in my own skin—or pretty much anywhere. But as I have gotten older, I have realized that none of us is supposed to feel completely at home in the world as it is now. Scripture itself affirms that the citizens of the next world are always, on some level, going to feel like "foreigners and strangers" in the present one. Why is this so? Because the citizens of heaven cannot shake their longing for their better, heavenly country.[3]

The very worst things about this present world can stir our longing for the world to come. The very best things about this present world can whet our appetites for the same. Appetizers do not satisfy like the feast does. Their purpose is not to fill us but to make us want more. The world is full of temporary wonder and heartache, but we were made for a world of everlasting fullness and joy. The world is full of pain, but we were made for a world of comfort. The world is full of hurt, but we were made for a world of happiness. The world is full of hate, but we were made for a world of love.

In this world, we feel what Scripture calls "the groan of creation" not because there is something wrong with us but because there is something right with us. Concerning the past, our species

---

3. Heb. 11:13–16.

hails from the garden of Eden, where humans were naked and had no shame, and who walked with God and each other and nature in perfect harmony and joy. But when sin and suffering came into the world, all of that got corrupted and became less than it was meant to be. Concerning the future, the redeemed among our species are destined for what Scripture calls the new heaven and new earth, where every person, place, and thing will be made new again by Jesus and "sickness, sorrow, pain, and death will be felt and feared no more."[4]

Because we are not Home yet, we still ache.

We're not freaks. Just damaged, hurting, and sick for Home. Homesick.

It's perfectly normal—or, better said, it's imperfectly and painfully normal—to feel uncomfortable in your own skin. It is normal to want to do what the turtles do when they crawl into a shell. You are not alone in that hard, sometimes hidden battle of yours. Neither am I in mine. Perhaps this is why John, the beloved disciple who seems so eager to convince us that we, too, are beloved in Christ, wrote, "By this we shall know that we are of the truth and reassure our heart before him; for whenever our heart condemns us, God is greater than our heart, and *he knows everything*. Beloved, if our heart does not condemn us, we have confidence before God."[5]

God knows everything—even the very worst, most humiliating, most devastating things about us. We are fully known by him and completely loved in Christ. We are always exposed before his eyes, yet never rejected. When we feel discomfort in

---

4. Samuel Stennett, arranged by Christopher Miner, "On Jordan's Stormy Banks" (public domain).

5. 1 John 3:19–21, emphasis mine.

our own skin, he comforts us with his dignity-restoring grace. When the noise of guilt, shame, regret, sorrow, awkwardness, and inadequacy torches our hearts with restless fire, he quiets us with what children's book writer Sally Lloyd-Jones calls his "Never Stopping, Never Giving Up, Unbreaking, Always and Forever Love."[6] He cannot love you more and he will not love you less, and there is nothing you will ever be able to do to change that.

Ever since that conversation at the dinner party, I have felt much better about being me. I have felt more comfortable about living in uncomfortable skin, and less awkward about feeling awkward. Why? Because the woman who said, "I don't like me," is someone I like a lot. I like her and want to be like her. She is a skilled and celebrated creative on weekdays. On nights and weekends, she is a dedicated wife, mother, grandmother, and churchwoman. She quietly serves and befriends underdogs and down-and-outers and is a loyal friend to many. She will give you the shirt off her back if you ask her to, and even if you don't. Though very successful, she shows no signs of being enamored with the sound of her own name. She is also quite funny.

One more thing about this friend from the dinner party. She is what some might call a "tortured artist." Every now and then, she will talk about how the source of her best creative work is a daily, low-grade feeling of anxiety and self-doubt. She has no idea how much her willingness to speak this truth means to me, her pastor and younger brother in the faith. As one who has a strange but unshakable affinity for Eeyore and the writer of Ecclesiastes, I need friends like this in my life, and this reminds me that others need people like me in theirs.

We Ecclesiastes types are not meant to go through life taking

6. Sally Lloyd-Jones, *The Jesus Storybook Bible* (Grand Rapids: ZonderKidz, 2007).

the wind out of everybody's sails. That is not our calling. God created us to be truth tellers, not soul crushers or life suckers. He puts us in people's lives to awaken them, not to exhaust them. That's why we need other people's optimism. Just as optimists need people like us in their circles, we also need optimists in ours. Those who love Philippians ("Rejoice in the Lord always! Again, I say, rejoice!") also need Ecclesiastes ("Everything is vapor!"). We can help each other see more clearly as we chip away at each other's blind spots and less developed personality traits. Community is how we grow.

If we have the patience for it, even people who don't naturally like each other can grow to love each other. And in loving each other, we also learn to like and need each other more and more over time. Joyful types learn to sing and savor songs of lament, and lamenting types learn to sing and savor songs of joy. Some people call this a rare kind of friendship. Other people call it church.

More on the "singing each other's songs" part in a moment.

~~~

But first we need somber books like Ecclesiastes because the joy of the Lord is amplified in the presence of lament. As my close friend and colleague Russ Ramsey once said in a sermon, lament is a necessary skill in the art of rejoicing.

Lament is a skill, and rejoicing is an art form. I like how that sounds. Don't you?

Most of us are familiar with the concept of the spoiled malcontent. Some of us may know a spoiled malcontent or two, and some of us may be one ourselves. The spoiled malcontent does almost nothing but moan, groan, and complain about things that other people count as blessings. This is not the same as lament. Even the writer of Ecclesiastes keeps his lamenting in check by affirming that there are also seasons for healing, building up, laughing, dancing, embracing, loving, and enjoying the peace that comes from God. Even with darkness as his undercurrent, he recognizes that it is *good* to eat with joy and drink with a happy heart, to enjoy life with one's spouse, and to perform one's work with zeal and passion.[7] Though he does not hesitate to name the harder things about life, the harder things are not the only things that he is willing to name. The spoiled malcontent, on the other hand, refuses to name anything except his or her dissatisfaction with virtually everything. For the spoiled malcontent who has many things to be thankful for, the glass isn't half empty. As he or she sees it, the glass is just *empty*.

Malcontents are, according to C. S. Lewis, in grave danger. He writes, "Hell begins with a grumbling mood, always complaining, always blaming others . . . but you are still distinct from it. You may even criticize it in yourself and wish you could stop it. But there may come a day when you can no longer. Then there will be no you left to criticize the mood or even to enjoy it, but just the grumble itself, going on forever like a machine. It is not a question of God 'sending us' to hell. In each of us there is something growing, which will BE hell unless it is nipped in the bud."[8]

Why do spoiled malcontents exist? First and foremost, they exist because sin exists. Entitlement and ingratitude are lodged

---

7. Eccl. 3:1–8; 9:7–10.
8. C. S. Lewis, *Mere Christianity*, revised and enlarged (New York: HarperOne, 2009), Kindle.

deeply within every human heart, waiting for an opportunity to express themselves. Spoiled malcontents set loose that ingratitude frequently, if not constantly.

Second, spoiled malcontents exist—at least many of them do—because their postures of entitlement and ingratitude have been nurtured by others. They have *been* spoiled. Many have not been sufficiently mentored, led, or loved toward the truth that life's blessings are gifts to be thankful for, not entitlements that we deserve. These blessings have not been earned by being God's or somebody else's "choice" people but are received because we have been "chosen" as undeserving yet beloved objects of God's or somebody else's generosity and grace. The only way to unspoil a spoiled malcontent is to help him or her see that on the other side of every blessing, there is a curse or two from which the blessing is sparing us.

I once took a good night's sleep for granted. But now that I have chronic insomnia, a good night's sleep—on those rare occasions when it happens—has become one of life's most wonderful, surprising, and unexpected gifts. I once took a bacon cheeseburger and a pile of fries with ketchup for granted. It used to be my almost-everyday lunchtime go-to. But now that I have high cholesterol, a very occasional greasy splurge goes down like a five-star feast. I once took the winter snow for granted. But now that I live in a city where it *really* snows only once or twice per decade, a bright-white, chilled blanket over the front yard and around the neighborhood strikes me as one of the world's greatest wonders.

Abundance can be appreciated only when seen in contrast to the world's scarcity, blessings to the world's curses, newness to the world's decay, or joy to the world's sorrows. The light of day is welcomed when experienced in contrast to the dark of night, the rush of victory to the agony of defeat, or the pleasures of leisure to the toils of hard work.

And then there is the kingdom of God and the promise of heaven. The weight of even the horrors of suffering in this world is lightened only in comparison with the eternal weight of God's glory and goodness found in the happiness of heaven. As C. S. Lewis thoughtfully observed, "That is what mortals misunderstand. They say of some temporal suffering, 'No future bliss can make up for it' not knowing that Heaven, once attained, will work backwards and turn even that agony into a glory."[9] The words of a hymn by Sir Thomas Moore bring added comfort: "Earth has no sorrow that heaven cannot heal."[10]

9. C. S. Lewis, *The Great Divorce* (New York: HarperOne, 2009), Kindle.
10. Sir Thomas Moore, "Come Ye, Disconsolate" (public domain, 1779–1852).

HONEST SONGS

D istressed feelings are underrated.

What if we practiced expressing our distressed feelings more freely? Would it be such a bad thing to give our distress the space and validity that we offer to our more joyful expressions?

Herman Melville called Ecclesiastes "the truest of all books" because the author, whom Melville presumed to be Solomon, told the raw and unvarnished truth about life as he understood and *felt* it to be. Like a skilled songwriter or poet, Solomon made sure that what was genuinely inside of him also came out of him. Melville likened Solomon to Jesus, whom the Bible also describes as a man of sorrows, acquainted with grief.[1]

This same Jesus is also pictured in Scripture as a Suffering Servant who learned obedience—and with it, faithfulness and joy—through the things that he suffered.[2]

What unsettles us most about the concept of a kingly servant who suffers is that it does not fit the triumphal American grid. The Suffering Servant fully embraces, and is careful not to diminish, dystopian stories as well as the happily-ever-after ones. He has no time for pretense or posing, for faking fine, for pretending that anxiety and depression, memories of childhood trauma, racism, and cancer are small concerns. He refuses to whitewash the darker parts of our history. He refuses to hide the truth, to sweep dirt under the rug, or to silence the invasive discomfort

---

1. Isa. 53:3.
2. Isa. 53:11; Heb. 5:8.

of our own or other people's lamenting. To the contrary, the Suffering Servant invites, even welcomes, our expressions of gut-churning honesty and bold expressions of sorrow.

The Suffering Servant invites us, in our pain, to wipe disingenuous smiles off our faces and start living honestly concerning how damaged and hurt we feel. He commands that we be righteously angry and that we hate what is evil, even as we cling to what is good.[3] Jesus models the same as he flips over tables in the temple and gets raging-bull furious about death.[4] Why does he get furious? Because death is no friend to him or to us. It is an enemy, an aggressor, a bully, and a vandal against human life and flourishing. Jesus loves humans, and when the humans you love become injured or threatened, the natural and godlike response is to get angry and feel the swell of energy directed toward righting a wrong.

Living honestly may also involve tears. Jesus wept and he welcomes us to do the same. "Weep with those who weep," says the Lord. "Live in harmony with one another. Do not be haughty, but associate with the lowly."[5]

There is a solidarity to suffering that we are meant to embrace, so that no one might suffer alone. There is a reason why people say misery loves company. Sharing in one another's suffering binds us together in the deepest form of fellowship. It mysteriously draws us closer to the fellowship of Jesus' suffering as we, together, become like him in his death.[6]

Almost every book of the Bible was written by a sufferer. Slaves from the misery of their oppression, prisoners from the stench of

---

3. Ps. 4:4; Eph. 4:26; Rom. 12:9.
4. Matt. 21:12–13; John 11:33.
5. John 11:35; Rom. 12:15–16.
6. Phil. 3:10.

their jail cells, refugees from the vulnerability of their homeless-ness, exiles from the haunting memory of their captors' brutality, adulterous and murderous and found-out kings from the horror of their guilt, and wealthy, successful, lacking-for-nothing kings who have been awakened to the harsh reality that everything is vapor.

These writers include sufferers like Moses, Daniel, Jonah, David, Solomon, and Paul. If you don't already have a good study Bible,[7] consider purchasing one and familiarizing yourself with their stories. Their pain, anxiety, and self-doubt was real and unrelenting, and their God gave them hope and endurance that carried them through. It doesn't sound very American, but it is how God has, in his great wisdom, designed things to work in a fallen world that has not been renewed and renovated yet.

Yet.

Because he loves, understands, and cares for us, God has also given us songs with which to express our sorrow together. Starting with the Psalms, which are God's original hymnbook for his people, he gives voice and platform to the full range of human, image-bearing emotion. Perhaps surprisingly, the psalms contain an abundance of lyrics that sound more like complaining, demandingness, dissatisfaction, anguish, anger, and protest than rejoicing.

In the spirit of Eeyore and Ecclesiastes, the psalmists cry, "How long, O LORD? Will you forget me forever? . . . Out of the depths I cry to you, O LORD! . . . I pour out my complaint before him; I tell my trouble before him . . . there is none who takes notice of me; no refuge remains to me; no one cares for my soul . . . Attend to my cry, for I am brought very low! Deliver me

---

7. One good option is the NIV *Biblical Theology Study Bible* edited by D. A. Carson et al.

from my persecutors . . . Bring me out of prison . . . In my distress I called to the LORD . . . My God, my God, why have you forsaken me? Why are you so far from saving me, from the words of my groaning? O my God, I cry by day, but you do not answer, and by night, but I find no rest."[8]

Have you ever prayed this way? Have you ever dared to register your deepest complaints, disappointments, and betrayed feelings to God? If not, why not? Maybe it's time to start. What is stopping you from doing so? Do you think that God cannot handle it or, worse, would reject you for it? Do you think he would be hurt or offended if you start praying these words—*his own words*—back to him?

Or maybe it isn't how God might respond that scares you. Maybe you are more afraid of yourself than you are of God's response to your unfiltered expressions of distress. Maybe you don't feel ready to face the pain that is inside you, to admit it, to get honest about it—to wipe the disingenuous smile off your face and start getting real. Real is unsettling, scary, even traumatic.

Take the risk anyway and lean in.

Leaning into lament is a necessary skill in the art of rejoicing. The psalmists affirm this to be true by their own Holy Spirit–inspired examples. It is not despite their faith but because of their faith that they pray with such honest, gutsy, raw, distressed emotion. And with their prayers they are inviting us—God is inviting us—to join them in their songs of joy *and* their songs of lament, to sing with them in a major key *and* to sing with them in a minor key, to express our happiness *and* to express our hurt.

Sometimes the parts of the Bible we should pay attention to

---

8. Ps. 13:1; 130:1; 142:2, 4, 6–7; 120:1; 22:1–2.

the most, and the parts of the psalms we should pray the most, are the parts that we have decided *not* to highlight or underline.

Remember that Ecclesiastes needs Philippians, and Philippians needs Ecclesiastes. Realism needs hope, and hope needs realism.

Neither is ever complete without the other.

Speaking of music, my friend and ministry colleague Kevin Twit has done masterful work over the years reviving old, forgotten hymn texts by pairing them with more accessible and modern melodies.

Kevin and his wife, Wendy, minister faithfully among students at Belmont University in our hometown of Nashville. Like their fellow Reformed University Fellowship (RUF) colleagues at other campuses worldwide, Kevin and Wendy have devoted themselves to getting *all* of the Bible's truth into young-adult minds, hearts, and lives. Many of their students are at Belmont because of its renowned music department, with the hope of becoming professional songwriters and musicians.

As part of his ministry, and as a skilled musician himself, Kevin has unearthed and introduced to his students a vast archive of rich, mostly ancient hymn texts over the years. Some of the musically inclined among them paired these texts with fresh, creative, singable melodies. Over time, the number of revitalized hymns became robust enough to produce an album, and then a second, and then a third, and many more. These revitalized hymns continue to be sung on college campuses and in churches around the world. Our church is among many who benefit from their meaningful work known as Indelible Grace. If you are familiar with and appreciate the music of artists like Sandra McCracken, Andrew Osenga, Dan Haseltine, Jeremy Casella, and Matthew Smith—to name only a few—much of their formation as musicians and songwriters took place under the Twits' shepherding and mentoring. Among the lyrics that have been popularized by these and other artists are:

- "O come and mourn with me awhile, O come ye to the Savior's side. O come, together let us mourn . . . O break, O break, hard heart of mine! Thy weak self-love and guilty pride His Pilate and His Judas were: Jesus our Lord is crucified."[9]
- "Guide me, O Thou great Jehovah, pilgrim through this barren land. I am weak, but Thou art mighty; hold me with Thy powerful hand . . . bid my anxious fears goodbye."[10]
- "Come, ye sinners, poor and wretched, weak and wounded, sick and sore; Jesus, ready, stands to save you, full of pity, joined with power . . . Come, ye weary, heavy laden, bruised and broken by the fall; if you tarry 'til you're better, you will never come at all . . . none but Jesus can do helpless sinners good."[11]

One Sunday in church, we sang a John Newton hymn that had been put to fresh melody by Kevin and the Indelible Grace artists. It is a hymn of lament and trust called "I Asked the Lord," in which Newton describes how God almost drove him

---

9. Frederick William Faber, arranged by Eric Ashley, "O Come and Mourn with Me Awhile" (public domain).

10. William Williams, arranged by Jeremy Casella, "Guide Me O Thou Great Jehovah" (public domain).

11. Joseph Hart, arranged by Matthew Smith, "Come Ye Sinners" (public domain).

to despair, made him feel the hidden evils of his heart, let the angry powers of hell assault his soul, aggravated his woe, laid him low, and broke his schemes of earthly joy. According to Newton, the reason God did all these things was to drive the minister to his knees to seek the help of God. All of these trials, it turns out, were God's answer to Newton's prayer to "grow in faith and love and every grace" and to "more of [God's] salvation know and seek more earnestly his face."[12]

After the service that Sunday, Kevin, who attends our church, told me that of all the old hymns that Indelible Grace has repopularized over the years, "I Asked the Lord" is the hands-down favorite among university students. I asked him why he thought this was so, and he said it is because the song is honest.

Honest. The song does not sugarcoat the truth that all humans, including American ones between the ages of eighteen and twenty-two, are fighting a hard, sometimes hidden battle.

Kevin then said, "We need to give our people more honest songs to sing, don't you think? I'm all in favor of songs that highlight the joy of the Lord. But everyone in the pews is hurting in some way, also. We need to give them more honest songs to sing." When he said this, it made me wonder if the triumphal American church, in some ways, has become a product of triumphal American culture.

Almost every person is insecure and underencouraged.[13]

Almost no person wants to admit it.

American culture, like many of our American churches, does not always value honest expressions of pain, sorrow, and distress. Most of us encounter the greeting, "How are you?" several times

---

12. John Newton, "I Asked the Lord," *Olney Hymns* (public domain, 1779).
13. I first heard this phrase from Dr. Michael Easley.

per week from family, friends, and colleagues. Not wanting to be a drag, we diminish and hide our hurt with a "turn that frown upside down" attitude. We answer, "I'm fine," as a standard reply, when in fact we are everything but fine. Somehow we must figure out a way to disentangle our legitimate hurt from the hiding impulse that is brought on by toxic shame.

When Christians say yes to positive, happy feelings but no to distressed feelings that reveal our hurt, we risk becoming carbon copies of a culture that is prone to sweep pain under the rug. In doing so, we become codependent relationally, and anemic spiritually and emotionally. Expressing distressed emotion in a broken world is a sign not of weak faith but of strong faith. It is a sign not of spiritual immaturity but of spiritual maturity. It is a sign not that we are unlike Christ but that we are like Christ. It is not a sign of weakness but a sign of strength.

When Israel forsook the Lord to worship false gods of their own imagination or broke the Sabbath, Yahweh got angry.[14] When the scribes and Pharisees leveraged the Sabbath to boast in their own righteousness and treat others with contempt, Jesus got angry.[15] When Jesus' friend Lazarus died, he got furious and wept.[16] When God's children stew in bitterness or participate in slander, raging anger, or malice, the Holy Spirit feels a deep, exacting grief.[17] When Jesus was about to die for the sins of the world, he felt scared. In his distress, he cried out, "My Father, if it be possible, let this cup pass from me; nevertheless, not as I will, but as you will."[18]

---

14. Ex. 32:1–10; Neh. 13:18.
15. Mark 2:22–28.
16. John 11:35.
17. Eph. 4:30–32.
18. Matt. 26:39.

The psalmists and Jesus felt pain, and they didn't hold it back.

We *rejoice* in the Lord, with the psalmists and Jesus as our guides. We also *lament* in the Lord, with the psalmists and Jesus as our guides, along with the writer of Ecclesiastes, Job, Jacob, Hannah, Mary, Paul, and many others. We affirm God's goodness when we let him make us happy. We also affirm his goodness when we let him make us sad.

Laughter is God's gift to us. So are our tears.

The call to rejoice in the Lord is not negated by our expressions of distress; it is honored and made complete by them. Our cries of anguish do not make us less human but make us more human. Our tears and our sorrows, as well as our courage to acknowledge that in this present world "everything is vapor," are in fact noble expressions of protest, fueled by a longing for things to return to *shalom* or God's true and irreversible peace, marked by the comprehensive and forever flourishing of every person, place, and thing. Shalom will be accomplished when every square inch of his universe is made whole, never to be tarnished or compromised or corrupted or diminished again.

Our displays of distress, far from dishonoring our God, honor him as our Creator and Redeemer, who "comes to make his blessings flow far as the curse is found."[19] Our cries and holy roars are for the return and completion of these promised realities. Our longing is for happily ever after, but not the ones we find in wishful, fictitious fairy tales. Our longing is for *the* Happily Ever After that is also true because it is rooted in time-space history and sealed by our Lord's resurrection from the dead and promised return.

The fact that Jesus will come again is our reason to rejoice.

---

19. Isaac Watts, "Joy to the World" (public domain, 1719).

The fact that he has not done so yet is our reason to lament, weep, wail, and hope. Though full and unmitigated rejoicing will come in the morning, now is also a time for tears.

❧

Why make so much of the emotions most people spend their lives trying to stuff, avoid, and ignore? I think there are two chief reasons why. The first is that our sources of distress can often be traced back to the ways we try to replace God with other, lesser things.

As C. S. Lewis observes, "God made us: invented us as a man invents an engine. A car is made to run on petrol, and it would not run properly on anything else. Now God designed the human machine to run on Himself. He Himself is the fuel our spirits were designed to burn, or the food our spirits were designed to feed on. There is no other. That is why it is just no good asking God to make us happy in our own way without bothering about religion. God cannot give us a happiness and peace apart from Himself, because it is not there."[20]

God has made us for himself, and our hearts are restless until they find their rest in him.[21]

In every human heart, there is a God-shaped and God-sized hole. When we try to fill the hole with anything but God, the hole remains hungry and parched, because anything that is God shaped and God sized is bigger than the universe itself. That hole will never be filled, it will never be satisfied, until it is filled with God and God alone. But to fill it in that way, some other

---

20. C. S. Lewis, *Mere Christianity* (New York: HarperOne, 2009), Kindle.

21. A paraphrase of Augustine, *The Confessions of St. Augustine*, 1.1.1 (Overland Park: Digireads.com, 2015), Kindle.

things may have to be ejected to make room for him. This will not always be easy. It will sometimes feel painful, even traumatic.

To recover from addiction, an addict must go through a season of withdrawal and subsequent seasons of painful resistance to craving. The same is true of us when we are suffering because we have asked something besides God—sex, money, power, health, career, other people, a certain lifestyle, or even religion—to serve as our functional savior. But all these pseudosaviors to which we cling, all these idols that block our vision of and diminish our appetites for grace, must be contended with and, possibly, let go of for a long time or forever.

Idols are tricky because they are usually good things. But in our foolishness, we turn them into things we cannot live without. But when we think that we can't live without something, in truth we are no longer able to live with it. Like a fifth of whiskey for an alcoholic or a plate of ribs for a man with heart disease, idols promise on the surface to make things better for us. But in fact they will make things worse for us. The more we consume them in the short run, the more they will, in the long run, consume us.

Would you be willing to let go of a lesser treasure if it meant living nearer to Christ? Does the idea of losing your life in order that you may find it sound attractive to you? Is there an appeal to seeking first the kingdom of God and his righteousness that exceeds the appeal of seeking lesser, more temporal things? Is there a part of you that wants God more than the things God has given to you or that you have taken or withheld from him? Do you want to do something about it? If so, then prepare to take up your cross and experience sorrow. Never forget that the greatest person who ever lived was also a man of sorrows, acquainted with grief.[22]

---

22. Isa. 53:3.

As Scripture attests, "We have peace with God through our Lord Jesus Christ . . . we rejoice in hope of the glory of God. Not only that, but we rejoice in our sufferings, knowing that suffering produces endurance, and endurance produces character, and character produces hope, and hope does not put us to shame, because God's love has been poured into our hearts through the Holy Spirit who has been given to us."[23]

If our desire is to know God more fully, we must assume this belief and posture. This is the path that the Suffering Servant says we must take. There is no bypass road around the cross to get to the crown. There is no shortcut past Good Friday to get to Easter. There is no joy without a sorrow, no rejoicing without mourning, no comfort without distress, no rest without weariness, no gain without loss, no songs of joy without songs of lament, no rejoicing from Philippians without the vapor from Ecclesiastes.

Do you recognize these paradoxes in your story? Are you able to sing them in your songs?

Most of us won't be able to answer these questions until we have hit rock bottom. This was (and is) most certainly true in my case.

---

23. Rom. 5:1–5.

MY TWO
STRANGE FRIENDS

One day in my midtwenties while studying to become a pastor, I was alarmed to see a suicide note published in the local newspaper. It was written by a pastor. In his note, the pastor said, "God forgive me for not being any stronger than I am. But when a minister becomes clinically depressed, there are very few places where he can turn to for help . . . it feels as if I'm sinking farther and farther into a downward spiral of depression. I feel like a drowning man, trying frantically to lift up my head to take just one more breath. But one way or another, I know I am going down."

The deceased had been the promising young pastor of a large, thriving church in Saint Louis. Having secretly battled depression for a long time, and having sought help through prayer, therapy, and medication, his will to claw through yet another day was gone. In his darkest hour, the young promising pastor decided he would rather join the angels than continue facing demons for years to come. The signoff to his note, "Yours in the Name of Our Blessed Lord, Our Only Hope in Life and Death," brought a strange comfort, because grace covers all types of things, including self-harm and suicide. One can only imagine the deep compassion in Christ's heart when his beloved children lose their way like this. Yet for this aspiring pastor, grief and confusion felt more real than hope did.

Grief and confusion grew even larger when a second pastor, also from Saint Louis, asphyxiated himself to death because of a similar, secret depression.

The news of these two pastor suicides shook me. How could these men—both exemplary leaders who believed in Jesus, preached grace, and comforted others with gospel hope—end up losing hope for themselves?

I had also heard others teach that being a Christian and being depressed aren't supposed to go together. "Light always drives out darkness," these misguided teachers would say. "When you're believing the right things, peace and joy will always follow." In that same season, a worship song based on such teaching was released that became very popular among Christians. The lyrics confidently declared that in the Lord's presence, all our problems will disappear.

But when reality strikes, such teachings and songs hurt more than they help. Two faithful pastors, who prayed and sought solace from Scripture every day, who served their churches and cities and counseled people and preached grace, ended their lives. What drove them to do so was that in God's presence, their problems, curiously, did *not* disappear.

I, too, have battled anxiety and depression from time to time. My struggle with both has most often been more low grade than intense. But in one particular season, anxiety and depression flattened me physically, emotionally, and spiritually.

During those days, I could not fall asleep for two weeks straight. Even sleeping pills couldn't calm the adrenaline and knock me out, which only made things worse. At night I was fearful of the quiet, knowing I was in for another all-night battle with insomnia that I was likely to lose. The sunrise also frightened me, an unwelcome reminder that another day of impossible struggle was ahead of me. I lost 15 percent of my body weight in two months. I could not concentrate in conversations. I found no comfort in God's promises from Scripture. I couldn't bring myself to pray anything but "Please help," "Please end this," and "Why?"

According to a study conducted by Thom Rainer, circumstance-triggered anxiety and depression hit ministers at a disproportionally high rate. Because of the unique pressures associated with spiritual warfare, unrealistic expectations from congregants and oneself, unrestrained and unaccountable criticism and gossip toward and about ministers (especially in the digital age), failure to take time off for rest and replenishment, marriage difficulties, financial strains, and the problem of comparison with other ministers and ministries, Rainer says that ministers are set up as prime candidates for descent into an emotional abyss.[1]

The two pastors committed suicide because they could not imagine navigating the emotional abyss for another day. Both also suffered their affliction in silence, for fear of being rejected. The one who left the note said that if a pastor tells anyone about his depression, he will lose his ministry. People don't want to be pastored, taught, or led by a damaged person.

Or do they?

Maybe instead of labeling anxious and depressed people as damaged goods, we should learn from the psalms and Jesus and Paul about the biblical theology of weakness. Maybe we should

---

1. Thom S. Rainer, "Pastors and Mental Health," *Charisma Leader*, March 3, 2014, https://ministrytodaymag.com/leadership/personal-character/20758-thom-rainer-pastors-and-mental-health/.

start learning how to apply that theology in our lives and also in the lives of those who are called to lead us. Even the apostle Paul said that it is in weakness that we experience the glory, power, and grace of God. This is how God works. God is upside down to our sensibilities. Better said, we are upside down to his.

❧

I once heard someone say that it's okay to realize that you are crazy and very damaged, because all the best people are. Like nothing else, suffering has a way of equipping us to be the best expressions of God's compassion and grace. It has a way of equipping us to love and lead in ways that are helpful and not harmful. A healer who has not been afflicted is extremely limited in his ability to participate in the healing of others. As Henri Nouwen has written, "The great illusion of leadership is to think that man can be led out of the desert by someone who has never been there."[2]

Conversely, she who has been afflicted is strangely strengthened in her ability to lead others into the less arid, more fertile, healing pastures of God.

The apostle Paul encourages us with these words: "Blessed be the God and Father of our Lord Jesus Christ, the Father of mercies and God of all comfort, who comforts us in all our affliction, so that we may be able to comfort those who are in any affliction, with the comfort with which we ourselves are comforted by God. For as we share abundantly in Christ's sufferings, so through Christ we share abundantly in comfort too. If we are afflicted, it is for your comfort and salvation; and if we are comforted, it is for your comfort, which you experience when you

---

2. Henri Nouwen, *The Wounded Healer* (Melbourne: Image Publishing, 2013), 72.

patiently endure the same sufferings that we suffer. Our hope for you is unshaken, for we know that as you share in our sufferings, you will also share in our comfort."[3]

According to Scripture, the "crazy, very damaged" people are the ones through whom God did the greatest things. It is worth adding more examples to the ones given previously. Hannah had bitterness of soul over infertility and a broken domestic situation. Elijah felt so beaten down that he asked God to take his life. Job and Jeremiah cursed the day that they were born. David repeatedly asked his own soul why it was so downcast. Even Jesus, the perfectly divine human, lamented that his soul was overwhelmed with sorrow. He wept when his friend died. Each of these biblical saints was uniquely empowered by God to change the world—never in spite of their affliction, and always because of it and through it.

The likes of these are God's chosen instruments to bring truth, beauty, grace, and hope into the world. Many of the best therapists have themselves been in therapy. It's how God works.

If you have experienced anxiety and depression, I share this part of my story to remind you that there is no shame in having this or any other affliction. In fact, our afflictions may be the key to our fruitfulness as carriers of Jesus' love. What feels like the scent of death to us may end up becoming the scent of life for others as we learn to comfort others in their affliction with the comfort that we, in our affliction, have received from God.

Broken trees bear fruit, and I am one of those trees, bent and broken. In my darkest hour, in those months of facing into the abyss of anxiety and depression and a rapidly diminishing will to live, there were two people who put themselves on permanent call for me. These two carried me day and night, with constant

---

3. 2 Cor. 1:3–7.

reminders that though I was down, I was not out. Though I was afraid, I was not alone. Though I had been called upon by God to face some demons, I was surrounded by an angelic presence. Perhaps these two, also, were my guardian angels.

These two angels were my brother, Matt, and my wife, Patti. Both were outstanding healers because they were themselves wounded healers. Both had suffered with anxiety and depression, too. Having been bent and broken themselves, they helped me in my hour of need to find the straight path of hope again.

Being afflicted does not make you ineffective.

Being damaged does not mean that you are done.

Anxiety and depression can also, ironically, be occasions for hope. After I had served as pastor at Nashville's Christ Presbyterian Church for about two years, one of our members told me that he thought I was a gifted preacher and that he was entirely unimpressed by this fact. He told me that the moment he decided to trust me, the moment he decided that I was *his* pastor, was when I disclosed to the whole church that I have struggled with anxiety and depression and that I have needed therapy for many years.

In that very moment, it dawned on me: as a pastor and as a man, my afflictions may end up having greater impact than my preaching or my vision ever will. It is helpful to remember that nearly all of the psalms—and all the books of the Bible— were themselves written from dark, depressed, wrecked, and restless places.

Anxiety and depression are also invitations into Sabbath rest. When you are laid flat and there's nothing you can do except beg for help, Jesus meets you in that place. It is from there that he summons the weary and heavy laden and the wrecked and restless to come to him and learn from him, to see and savor his humility and gentleness of heart, that we might find rest for our souls.[4]

Our God is a tender God. He does not break bruised reeds.[5] Instead, he handles them with utmost care. This is true of every kind of bruise. Our guilt and regret trigger his forgiveness, moral cleansing, and welcome. Our hurt and sorrow trigger his maternal tenderness and paternal protection. Our fear and doubt trigger his reassuring mercy and care. And that is one way he reveals who he is. Or as it is put in The Lord of the Rings, "The hands of the king are the hands of a healer, and so shall the rightful king be known."[6]

For those who experience anxiety and depression, there is nothing quite like an easy yoke and a light burden under which to process the pain. Likewise, there is nothing quite like a king whose hands are healing hands.

Mental illness has been one way for God to remind me that being awesome is not my calling. He has not called me to be awesome or to crush it at life or to be spoken well of and liked or to be a Christian celebrity or hero. These competencies belong to Jesus and Jesus alone.

As for me, God has foremost called me to *be* loved, to be receptive *to* his love, and to find my rest *in* his love. He has called me to remember that because of Jesus, I already have a name. I will be remembered and celebrated and sung over even after I

---

4. Matt. 11:28–30.
5. Isa. 42:3.
6. J. R. R. Tolkien, *The Return of the King*, The Lord of the Rings (Boston: Houghton Mifflin Harcourt, 2012), Kindle.

am long gone, because he is my God and I am his person. He is my Father and I am his son. And on that day into eternity, there will be no more death, mourning, crying, or pain.

The story is told of a little girl who recited for her Sunday school teacher, "The Lord is my Shepherd; that's all I want." Sometimes the misquotes are the best and truest quotes, yes?

Kierkegaard said that the thorn in his foot enabled him to spring higher than anyone with sound feet. The apostle Paul said something similar about the thorn in his flesh. The thorn kept him from becoming prideful. It kept him humble. It kept him fit for God and fit for the people whom God had called him to love and serve. There is glory in weakness. There is a power that is made perfect in that place.[7]

Though I would not wish anxiety or depression on anyone, I am strangely thankful for the unique way that this affliction has led me, time and again, back into the rest of God.

As one of my mentors is fond of saying, "All you need is nothing. All you need is need."[8]

---

7. 2 Cor. 12:7–10.

8. I have heard Tim Keller use this phrase many times, both in sermons and in conversation.

THOUGH I DIE

I turned fifty-three this year, which means I am likely closer to the day of my death than I am the day of my birth.

Once a two-sport athlete whose days were filled with strength, determination, unlimited energy, and a marathon runner's resting heart rate, I am now more tired and less vibrant than I used to be. Part of that is because of insomnia, but it's also a function of getting older. Now more than ever, I feel what Albert Camus called "the bitter taste of the mortal state" and what the apostle Paul called "the groan of creation."

But even at fifty-three, some things remain constant. Easter's promise echoes every year and the Lord's Supper welcomes me every week. Before the Supper, our church family joins other saints around the world by reciting the truth that Christ has died, Christ has risen, and Christ will come again. These words are anchored in history. They are trustworthy and true, and present me with a paradox that is both troubling and hopeful: Though I die, yet shall I live.[1]

According to Scripture, when we die, we will not be buried in the dirt forever but will only be planted there for a time. Our mortal bodies, now tarnished by weariness, will be like fertile seeds in waiting. Once resurrected, our bodies will assume all the features of immortality, full redemption, unending momentum, untarnished flourishing, and imperishable bliss. We are now and

---

1. John 11:25.

forevermore united with Jesus who *is* the resurrection and the life. Because Jesus lives and will never die again, the same must be true of us.

It *must* be true, provided that we have received the gift of faith. Even the smallest amount of faith in Jesus is plenty. Why is this so? Because it is not the strength, nor the quality, nor the quantity of our faith that will get us Home. Rather, it is the strength, quality, and quantity of God's immeasurable goodness and grace and faithfulness that gets us Home.

Whether our faith is big or small, a constant or constantly needled with doubt, an arena for angst or a refuge for peace, a tiny mustard seed is all that's called for. It is not our fitness to be saved that seals our standing with Christ but his fitness to save us. It is not our repentance that leads him to be kind toward us but his kindness that leads us to be repentant toward him.[2] His kindness toward us is tender, gentle, and lowly in heart. At the same time, his kindness is filled with earth-shaking, death-defying power.

"Your brother will rise again," Jesus told the grieving and doubting Martha, still undone by the death and burial of her beloved brother and Jesus' beloved friend, Lazarus. "I am the resurrection and the life. Whoever believes in me, though he die, yet shall he live, and everyone who lives and believes in me shall never die. Do you believe this?"[3]

There is no more important question than this. Does Martha believe, do you believe, do I believe *this?*

---

2. Rom. 2:4.
3. John 11:23–26.

For those like me who are aging but also for those who are young, healthy, and less accustomed to entertaining thoughts about death and decline, Jesus' question for Martha is relevant right now. As I write this, the world is recovering from a global pandemic. Although we would all love nothing more than to put its decimating impact behind us, we are still in its cruel, harsh, and unrelenting wake. This unanticipated and lingering crisis has thrown nearly everything and everyone out of whack. Some have lost their job security and career prospects, others their health, others their community, others their sanity, and some their very lives. How disorienting that a microscopic organism could rock the landscape of our lives so quickly and drastically. It confirms, once again, that we are not in control. We never were in control, nor will we ever be.

A small few have survived the pandemic relatively unscathed. Some have even profited financially in it and even because of it. However, even the good fortune of the lucky ones will fade and perish in time. No one exits this world unscathed, untarnished, and unrattled—not Job with his great wealth, not David with his great conquests, not Solomon with his great splendor, not Hannah and Ruth and Mary with their great virtue, and not even Jesus with his great perfection. The breath you just took is one more toward your last. All new people in a hundred years. Life is wondrous and supremely difficult, and then we die. Nobody, even the author of life himself, gets to escape our last enemy, which is death.

Until some of us do escape it.

In a letter he wrote from prison while awaiting execution for opposing Hitler, Dietrich Bonhoeffer wrote that death is "the supreme festival on the road to freedom."[4]

---

4. Dietrich Bonhoeffer, *Letters and Papers from Prison* (New York: Touchstone, 2011), Kindle.

Welsh-born poet and priest George Herbert expressed similar hope when he said that death used to be an executioner, but the gospel makes it into a gardener. The following lines from his famous poem "Death" expound on this hopeful thought:

> Death, thou wast once an uncouth hideous thing,
> Nothing but bones,
> The sad effect of sadder groans . . .
>
> But since our Savior's death did put some blood
> Into thy face,
> Thou art grown fair and full of grace,
> Much in request, much sought for as a good.
>
> For we do now behold thee gay and glad,
> As at Doomsday;
> When souls shall wear their new array,
> And all thy bones with beauty shall be clad.
>
> Therefore we can go die as sleep, and trust
> Half that we have
> Unto an honest faithful grave;
> Making our pillows either down, or dust.[5]

In Christ, we possess a hope that transcends and ultimately defeats human mortality. Because his life, death, burial, resurrection, and promises are all trustworthy and true, an eternal "weight of glory" awaits us.

---

5. Helen Wilcox, ed., *George Herbert: 100 Poems* (Cambridge: Cambridge Univ. Press, 2016), 154.

As Scripture attests, "We do not lose heart. Though our outer self is wasting away, our inner self is being renewed day by day. For this light momentary affliction is preparing for us an eternal weight of glory beyond all comparison, as we look not to the things that are seen but to the things that are unseen. For the things that are seen are transient, but the things that are unseen are eternal."[6]

Any regret, hurt, fear, and subsequent weariness we experience today is a prelude to the lives we will enjoy, in complete absence of these and all other ills, in the coming new heaven and new earth. The current and coming chapters of our lives—including the ones that seem demoralizing or terminal—are but middle chapters in the Story of God. The final chapter, which still awaits us, has also been written and published and cannot be revised or deleted. It turns even the most tragic stories into the Happily Ever After Story that is actually true. It is world without end, an imperishable bliss that will put all that is bent, bruised, and broken into permanent rearview. It will be, as singer-songwriter Jeremy Casella has said, like death in reverse.

To our present and wearied selves, such promises feel more out of reach than they do real. Perhaps this is because the world that still is prevents us from fathoming the world that will be. Or perhaps we are more preoccupied with what must happen to us *first*, before those promised times of flourishing peace become our norm: "It is appointed for man to die once, and after that comes judgment."[7]

Death is, on the one hand, a formidable and brutal enemy. It is fierce, fracturing, and laden with heaviness. Even Jesus, the one who holds the power to conquer death, paused to grieve

---

6. 2 Cor. 4:16–18.
7. Heb. 9:27.

and weep and rage at what death had done to his beloved friend Lazarus and to the community of mourners it left in its wake. Jesus also registered wailing cries of pain and protest concerning his own death on the cross.

But the news surrounding death is not all bad for the people of God. Like the excruciating pain of labor and delivery before childbirth, like the darkness before the dawn, and like winter before springtime, the coldness and fury and pain of death is also a pathway to the kind of life we were made to have. Death is not the end for us but rather is the final leg of our bent, busted-up, guilt-gutted, hurt-hindered, fear-wearied existence in a fallen world. There is no bypass road around it. It cannot be avoided. To experience joy, abundance, and the freedom of unfettered, unrestrained, and uninterrupted life, we must first journey through death's dark valley. It is not only the wages of sin, which have already been covered on our account by Jesus, but is also a necessary byproduct of what Scripture calls the groan of creation, in which every person, place, and thing has been made subject, at least for now, to death and decay.[8]

So what is the good news here? The central motive of Christ's mission was love, which compelled him to lay down his life for our sakes. He did this to ensure for all God's people that death would die, burials would be buried, terminal conditions would be terminated, and endings would end. The good news: Jesus Christ conquered and rejected death with a holy rejection. He hates death with a holy hatred. There is comfort to be had in this. On the other side of death, all of us who are in Christ will be able, once and for all and forever, to put erosive and life-sucking vandals like death, mourning, crying, and pain in the rearview.

---

8. Rom. 8:18–25.

One of my faith heroes is a woman in her seventies named Joni. This remarkable soul has been paralyzed from the neck down since age seventeen because of a diving accident. She has also survived breast cancer, decades of chronic pain, and wearied seasons of praying, "Why, Lord, why?"

Joni is also among the most joyful, hopeful people I have ever known.

As a middle-aged man who is beginning to consider his own mortality, I need Joni's story and voice. I savor her influence in my life for many reasons, including her well-formed, well-lived, hard-fought belief that God takes the very worst things life throws at us—tragedy, fear, regret, weariness, and more—and turns them into good. I also savor the influence of her vivid, hope-filled vision of heaven that has been formed through her groaning. When asked why she thinks an all-loving, all-powerful God let her get cancer, Joni answered, "I've been drawn closer to the Savior, even with this breast cancer. There are things about His character that I wasn't seeing a year ago or even six months ago. That tells me I'm still growing and being transformed . . . When people ask about healing, I'm less interested in the physical and more interested in healing my heart. Pray that I get rid of my lazy attitude about God's Word and prayer, of brute pride—set me free from self-centeredness. Those are more important, because Jesus thought they were more important."[9]

---

9. Sarah Pulliam Bailey, "Joni Eareckson Tada on Something Greater Than Healing," *Christianity Today*, October 8, 2010, www.christianitytoday.com/ct/2010/october/12.30.html.

Once, I heard Joni give a talk in which she shared her belief that suffering fits into God's plan for our lives. From the confines of her wheelchair, she said that sometimes God permits what he hates in order to accomplish what he loves. You could have heard a pin drop.

Joni's words are simultaneously disturbing and comforting. Her perspective flows from a deep, abiding awareness of the cross of Jesus. At the cross, God permitted what he hates—the violent marring and murder of his only begotten and sinless Son, to accomplish what he loves—the salvation of sinners whom he loves *that* much, not because they are good but because he is.

In a related essay, Joni added the following concerning her wheelchair: "I sure hope I can bring this wheelchair to heaven . . . I hope to bring it and put it in a little corner . . . then in my new, perfect, glorified body, standing on grateful glorified legs, I'll stand next to my Savior . . . And I will say, 'Jesus, do you see that wheelchair? You were right when you said that in this world we would have trouble, because that thing was a lot of trouble. But the weaker I was in that thing, the harder I leaned on you. And the harder I leaned on you, the stronger I discovered you to be. It never would have happened had you not given me the bruising of the blessing of that wheelchair.' Then the real ticker-tape parade of praise will begin. And all of earth will join in the party."[10]

Strong souls like Joni's tend to emerge not from a life of surface comfort but from rock-bottom experiences. The most remarkable humans with the most remarkable faith are usually the ones who have come to the end of themselves, suffered deeply, and lost much.

---

10. John Piper and Justin Taylor, eds., *Suffering and the Sovereignty of God* (Wheaton, IL: Crossway, 2006), 203.

Beautiful people don't just happen. But when they do happen, even a wheelchair can become a pulpit, a chemo room a place of worship, chronic pain a path to holiness, burial dirt a plot of resurrection soil, and death a festival on the road to freedom.

For those of us who will never bear the burden of life in a wheelchair, Joni's perspective is an invitation to treat our other immobilizing and wearying realities as our own wheelchairs in which we can find, know, and limp with Christ toward freedom. If our hearts are open to receive it, even our regret can become a road on the festival to the freedom of God's forgiveness, grace, and welcome, our hurt to the freedom of God's tenderness, mercy, and healing hands, our fear to the freedom of God's reassuring presence and promises, and our subsequent weariness to the freedom of God's rest.

OF THE INCREASE

B ecause Christ has died, Christ has risen, and Christ will come again, our long-term worst-case scenario is *not* that we will rot in the ground. On the contrary, our long-term worst-case scenario is resurrection, everlasting life, and an ever-increasing, imperishable bliss. One hundred years, ten thousand years, and a thousand billion years from now, this is as bad as it will ever get for us. We can know this because it is written, "Of the increase of [the Suffering Servant, Jesus'] government and of peace there will be no end . . . the zeal of the LORD of hosts will do this."[1]

Of the increase. What did the prophet Isaiah mean when he wrote these words? What did the Holy Spirit mean when he inspired them?

The Beloved Disciple's vision, also inspired by the Holy Spirit, of Christ seated on his throne in the new heaven and new earth helps us understand what this "increase" means. John writes, "'Behold, the dwelling place of God is with man. He will dwell with them, and they will be his people, and God himself will be with them as their God. He will wipe away every tear from their eyes, and death shall be no more, neither shall there be mourning, nor crying, nor pain anymore, for the former things have passed away.' And he who was seated on the throne said, 'Behold, I am making all things new.' Also he said, 'Write this down, for these words are trustworthy and true.'"[2]

---

1. Isa. 9:7.
2. Rev. 21:1–5.

When Jesus says he is making all things new, the Greek verb tense is unmistakable. He is saying that in the coming new heaven and new earth, he will make all things new *continually*. He will never stop making all things new. Every single minute, hour, day, week, month, year, decade, century, and millennium—forever and ever and ever—will be better and fuller, more life giving and satisfying, than all of what has come before.

There is coming a day when we, his beloved children by faith, will feel younger, stronger, smarter, faster, happier, and more rested, tended to, and full hearted than we can even dream about currently. Our work will be fulfilling, even fun. Our play will be epic and unending. Our connection with God and each other will be a deep source of joy and fulfillment. Honesty will be effortless; deception, backbiting, and conflict will be impossible. Love will be the norm; hate, division, assuming the worst, echo chambers, and calling out to cancel will be distant memories.

We will be free forever in the empire of Jesus, which is what my friend, prayer partner, and fellow pastor Ray Ortlund calls the empire of grace: "The empire of grace will forever expand . . . [Jesus] will not come back to tweak this problem and that. He will return with a massive correction of all systemic evil forever . . . 'Of the increase' . . . forever ascending, forever enlarging, forever accelerating, forever intensifying. There will never come one moment when we will say, 'This is the limit. He can't think of anything new. We've seen it all.' No. The finite will experience ever more wonderfully the infinite, and every new moment will be better than the last."[3]

This sounds wonderful to me. Does it to you? Even if we

---

3. Raymond C. Ortlund Jr., *Preaching the Word: Isaiah—God Saves Sinners* (Wheaton, IL: Crossway, 2012), Logos.

struggle to believe, these words are forever and always trustworthy and true. It is the object of our faith, not the size of it, that will get us Home.

Because of Christ, in the life to come the abundance and flourishing we've always dreamed of will no longer be a dream. The regret, hurt, and fear that weary us today will be as a nightmare from which we have awakened. Like all other nightmares of the past, our future awakening will only increase our joy in the treasures of life. What we thought had been lost will be found, regained, and renewed.

As the apostle Paul said confidently in the face of persecution, suffering, and daily death threats, "In all these things we are more than conquerors through him who loved us. For I am sure that neither death . . . nor anything else in all creation, will be able to separate us from the love of God in Christ Jesus our Lord."[4] As those who share in the same inheritance as Paul, we too can embrace this hope in a future that is lovely and bright.

Dear sinning, suffering, Homesick friend, I pray God will give you confidence that your best days and years—your most golden, healthy, and happy adventures—are never behind and always ahead of you. In the new heaven and new earth, Jesus will continuously make all things new.

These things being trustworthy and true, I can think of no better last word for this last prelude, before "Chapter One and Only" begins, than the words of C. S. Lewis as he describes a healed Narnia under the reign of Aslan, the resurrected lion, whose triumph resembles the one we have come to know as the Lion of Judah: "And as He spoke, He no longer looked to them like a lion; but the things that began to happen after that were

---

4. Rom. 8:31–39.

so great and beautiful that I cannot write them. And for us this the end of all the stories, and we can most truly say they all lived happily ever after. But for them it was only the beginning of the real story. All their life in this world and all their adventures in Narnia had only been the cover and the title page: now at last they were beginning Chapter One of the Great Story which no one on earth has read: which goes on for ever: in which every chapter is better than the one before."[5]

---

5. C. S. Lewis, *The Last Battle* (New York: Harper Collins, 2008), Kindle.

THEN I SAW

Then I saw a new heaven and a new earth, for the first heaven and the first earth had passed away, and the sea was no more. And I saw the holy city, new Jerusalem, coming down out of heaven from God, prepared as a bride adorned for her husband. And I heard a loud voice from the throne saying, "Behold, the dwelling place of God is with man. He will dwell with them, and they will be his people, and God himself will be with them as their God. He will wipe away every tear from their eyes, and death shall be no more, neither shall there be mourning, nor crying, nor pain anymore, for the former things have passed away."

And he who was seated on the throne said, "Behold, I am making all things new." Also he said, "Write this down, for these words are trustworthy and true." And he said to me, "It is done! I am the Alpha and the Omega, the beginning and the end. To the thirsty I will give from the spring of the water of life without payment. The one who conquers will have this heritage, and I will be his God and he will be my son."

—Revelation 21:1–7

Beloved, we are God's children now, and what we will be has not yet appeared; but we know that when he appears we shall be like him, because we shall see him as he is.

—1 John 3:2

The End,
and the True Beginning.
World without end. Amen.

BONUS MATERIAL

Key Quotes

If you like to share book quotes on social media or otherwise, or if you just appreciate having key quotes all in the same place, here is a collection from *Beautiful People Don't Just Happen*:

From Prologue 1

"There is a bright blue sky of forgiveness and grace for demoralized, defeated souls. The air space is unlimited and free. Freedom is what God wants for us."

"Through pain and sorrow, I have been tutored in the counterintuitive nature of [God's] ways. I have learned that the greatest strength comes through the avenue of weakness, the greatest wisdom through the avenue of disorientation, the greatest joy through the avenue of sorrow, and the greatest worship through the avenue of doubt."

"The human soul under the disciplined regimen of God works like muscles do under the disciplined regimen of a trainer. The more the soul is worked and stretched to its limits, the more able it becomes to endure suffering and enjoy God all at once."

"True words are more easily received and metabolized when offered in a setting of empathy, understanding, and love."

"We are not Home yet. That's the hard news. The hopeful news is that Home awaits."

From Prologue 2

"Many Christians have been drawn into the abyss of turning party platforms into their doctrine, pundits into their prophets, and politicians into their Jesus. Outrage is at an all-time high, and some people are at the end of their wits."

"Every person you meet is fighting a hard, hidden battle."

"No matter how hard we try to make it so, this present world refuses to be our paradise. We cannot make heaven happen for ourselves because heaven can only be given and received. When we accept and receive this truth, the revival of our hearts is made more possible."

"Many of the world's greatest souls became their best selves not in spite of but because of their own distress."

"Beautiful people. The ones we admire. The ones who change the world for good. The ones we like and want to be like. These people do not 'just happen.'"

"So many of the books—both Old Testament and New—were authored by someone who was enslaved, seeking asylum, in prison, facing persecution, or under another form of distress."

"Sometimes the deepest, truest faith feels more like defeat than it does victory."

From Prologue 3

"God's better-than-ness dwarfs our trophies and promotions. God's stronger-than-ness dwarfs our muscle and achievement. God's Godness dwarfs our perches of human pride."

"There is an even bigger mountain that the tiniest bit of faith can move—the mountain of the human heart . . . The greatest mountain to be moved is a needy, tired heart that won't run to Jesus except as a last resort. All you need is nothing; all you need is need."

"God is tuned in to the worst things about you and still loves you."

"Would you dare to believe that God does not hate you? That he sees you at your worst and loves you no less? That if you confess your sins, sorrows, and fears to him right now, you will not be cremated but healed?"

"Would you dare believe that your own regret, hurt, and fear—your not-enough-ness—is not a barrier to God's healing mercy but the very occasion for it?"

"If ever you're tempted to hate yourself, be careful. It is a grievous thing to hate a child whom God cannot stop loving."

From Prologue 4

"We miss out on the best things because we prefer the lesser things. We miss out on the wondrous things because we prefer the humdrum things. We miss out on the adventure because we prefer the safe, contained, controllable things. Gazing at beauty is its own reward. Looking away from beauty is its own punishment."

"Whether now or later, our hearts are bound to get blistered by grief."

"The world is both exquisite and terrible."

"It is a miracle that Jesus endured the cross of death 'for the joy set before him.' It is also a miracle when other frail humans like ourselves can do the same."

From Prologue 5

"Keeping our lamps filled with oil—a metaphor for ordering our lives around *knowing Jesus* through worship with a local church, regular Bible study, and prayer (what some call the formative 'spiritual disciplines')—is imperative for survival when our day of darkness comes."

"If your story includes anxiety, you know what it is like to grow weary from meditating on imagined worst-case scenarios. I'm here to tell you, there is no sustained way to confront those scenarios without the presence of a steadily nourished, full reservoir of biblical truth."

"The long-term *worst* case scenario is that all sad and hurtful things will come untrue. Just as certain as Christ's empty tomb is this: We too will rise from death's dark into a world where every day will be better than the one before."

"Don't underestimate the power of formative habit. What you take into you is what will come out of you when the days of trouble come."

"Abiding in Christ, who is the light of the world, is your safeguard from getting lost in the dark."

"We use our fingers to write notes, brush hair out of our eyes, tie a shoe, scratch an itch, floss teeth. But God? God uses *his* fingers to create, sustain, and govern square inches as well as whole continents, heads of hair as well as whole populations, tiny particles as well as unseen galaxies."

"Jesus, the Maker of the moon and the stars, stoops to wash your dirty, tired, demoralized feet."

"Jesus will come again—this time not to defeated followers in a remote region but in unmistakable power and a glory so weighty and expansive, and with the inauguration of a future so bright, that it makes a dying man want to wear happy socks."

From Prologue 6

"Jesus takes center stage as the Hero in the happily-ever-after Fairy Tale that is also true."

"In our singing, we delight in the goodness, beauty, love, and excellencies of God. We also delight in and spur on one another's enrichment and flourishing."

"For as long as I have been a pastor, I have noticed that every time we sing 'It Is Well' in church, the ones who sing the loudest are the sufferers."

"Being a daughter or son of God is a gift granted by his grace and mercy alone. It has nothing to do with our opinion of our worthiness. We are welcomed, embraced, and kept by him on our best days and our worst days, when we succeed and when we fail, when we love him and when we resent him, when we receive him and when we resist him, when we are pursuing him and when we are avoiding him. This is why he calls himself our Father, as opposed to our fair-weather friend. This is why he relates to us not on the basis of a contract but of a covenant."

"God's love for us is consistent not because of the fickle goodness that is in us but because of the familial and fatherly goodness that is in him."

"[God] cannot love you more and he will not love you less. There is nothing you will ever be able to do to change this."

From Prologue 7

"[God] breathes life into us as he tends to us in our weakest, most humiliating, and most vulnerable places. He lifts us up off the ground and invites us to sing of his love, step onto the dance floor, and take our honored seat at the marriage feast."

"[God's] answer to our sin is not condemnation but grace. His answer to our shame is not rejection but tenderness. His answer to our repeat failures is not last-straw cancelation but never-ending embrace. His answer to our slowness to listen is not disgusted retreat but pursuing kindness. His answer to the grossest things about us is not to shout us down and shut us out but to quiet us with his love."

"Have you ever stopped and marveled at how the Bible, including God's chosen family, is filled to the brim with screwups? This is my favorite thing about the Bible. All the screwups that are in there."

"If God is going to do anything good through human beings, he will have to do so in spite of compromised ethics, mixed motives, and hypocritical realities."

"It is impossible to be a Christian and *not* be a hypocrite, if by hypocrite we mean someone who lives inconsistently with who they claim to be and what they claim to believe. But our hypocrisy does not negate our Christian faith. Instead, our hypocrisy establishes it."

"We are not saintly people who have earned our place. Rather, we are sinful people who have been saved by grace."

"If God only worked with people who are not hypocrites, he would have no one to work with besides Jesus."

"A broken hallelujah is still a hallelujah. In the ears of God, it is a sweet sound."

"It's impossible to be too much of a sinner for church, because the church is *for* sinners and sinners only . . . church has nothing to offer to those who don't believe themselves to be sinners. The same is true of Jesus."

"Sometimes if you give Jesus one inch of your trust, he will respond by giving you a hundred miles of love and affection. Sometimes if you give Jesus one thimbleful of pleading, he will return to you an ocean full of compassion and care."

"Everything in us that has been lost can be found again."

From Prologue 8

"Hitting bottom, if we survive it, awakens us to the fact that we never grow past our need for healing. Admitting we are frail and incomplete is not a sign of weakness but a sign of strength. It's what makes the healing possible."

"Admitting self-defeat is key to successful recovery. It involves raw honesty about your worst qualities and the destructive decisions you have made. It requires you to make amends with those who have suffered because of your choices. Recovery is built on the foundation of embracing weakness and your lack of control, which is the first essential step to getting well."

"For God to be known truly, he must reveal himself to us, not be created or recreated by us. He must do all the censoring, revising, and correcting to align us to himself. We are unwise when we attempt to relate to him in the reverse."

"We don't really believe that to err is human, because our hearts tell us we should be perfect—as if the law of God were somehow already written on our hearts."

"Our failure to measure up even to our own standards leaves us feeling defensive, ashamed, and prone to medicate and hide. It makes us bristle at things like scolding, shaming, and condemning, while also—and ironically—turning us into people who scold, shame, and condemn."

"Like anyone else, we pastors believe and we doubt. We listen patiently and we lose our tempers, we give selflessly and we act selfishly, we preach and we gossip, we pray and we sometimes cuss. We can be kind and hurtful, hopeful and cynical, tender and abrasive, loving and hateful, courageous and cowardly, faithful and frail, hardworking and lazy. Even at our best, we are a duplicitous bunch."

"Why do we bully others? Is it not because we are terrified ourselves of being crushed? Why do we act so big toward our frail and imperfect human peers? Is it not because on the inside, we feel invisibly small?"

"Self-esteem is overrated. Only an esteem that comes from beyond us—from the forgiveness, acquittal, and favor achieved for us on the cross—will be able to help, hold, and sustain us."

"Rejoice. You are a train wreck. You are also more loved than you ever dreamed."

From Prologue 9

"Some people believe that words like sin, guilt, judgment, wrath, and confession don't belong in the human vocabulary anymore. Such words seem regressive, arcane, primitive, unsophisticated, unenlightened. Too negative, morose, depressing, defeating. But are they?"

"The grace and love of Jesus confirm that he is invitingly approachable. The truth and law of Jesus confirm that he can also be transcendent and dangerous."

"The most 'disabled' among us are the ones who lack self-awareness and experience no guilt. At least those who admit their guilt know there is a better version of themselves to wish for and become."

"When sin ceases to be wretched, grace ceases to be amazing."

"Some days, I feel less holy and virtuous than I did when I first believed in Christ. Some days, I feel more fraudulent in my faith than authentic, more disingenuous than real, more bent than straight."

"The more mature we become *in* Christ, the deeper we will feel our need *for* Christ. The stronger our faith in Christ becomes, the weaker in ourselves we will feel. 'The feel of faith is not strength but dependent weakness.'"

"It is good to be reminded often that God has bad taste. That he welcomes even—no, especially—the wretched into his circle, family, and heart."

"God reserves special attention and tender loving care for those who know that they miss the mark. Likewise, he takes issue with those who think of themselves as morally superior, popular, shiny, rich, well networked, or intelligent. This is no doubt why morally upright people can be so difficult to reach with the message of Christ while morally flattened people are often easier to reach."

"Weary sinners have no energy left for . . . fakery. Instead, they receive every truthful word with thanks, especially the ones who declare that God is good and they are not."

"Jesus welcomes and receives us not despite the worst things about us but because of them. His favorite thing to do is to *undo* our self-inflicted regret with his grace, tend to our self-inflicted hurt with his mercy, and quiet our self-inflicted fear with his love. That's who he is, and that is what he does."

"I am able to know [Christ] best in the context of safe, accountable community."

From Prologue 10

"If the Bible is a party, then Ecclesiastes is the party pooper."

"No human soul was made to bear the weight of fame except the soul of Jesus. Jesus alone has the character and capacity to stand on a pedestal and not get crushed by it."

"We humans—all of us—are meant to worship versus being worshiped, to stand in awe versus having others stand in awe of us, to bow the knee versus being bowed unto, to exalt Christ's fame and fortune versus seeking our own fame and fortune."

"Intimacy cannot happen without honesty."

"Life is tragic, and then we die. This is the plain, unfiltered truth about the universe and us. None can escape it. Everything is vapor. Everyone is leaking. The wages of sin is death."

From Prologue 11

"When we bring our sorrows out of hiding, hope follows closely behind. Admitting and owning the diagnosis, it turns out, is the first step in the direction of healing."

"I don't always feel at home in my own skin . . . or pretty much anywhere. But as I have gotten older, I have realized that none of us is supposed to feel completely at home in the world as it is now."

"The world is full of temporary wonder and heartache, but we were made for a world of everlasting fullness and joy. The world is full of pain, but we were made for a world of comfort. The world is full of hurt, but we were made for a world of happiness. The world is full of hate, but we were made for a world of love."

"Because we are not Home yet, we still ache. We're not freaks. Just damaged, hurting, and sick for Home. Homesick."

"Even people who don't naturally like each other can grow to love each other . . . Joyful types learn to sing and savor songs of lament, and lamenting types learn to sing and savor songs of joy. Some people call this a rare kind of friendship. Other people call it church."

"The only way to unspoil a spoiled malcontent is to help him or her see that on the other side of every blessing, there is a curse or two from which the blessing is sparing us."

"Abundance can be appreciated only when seen in contrast to the world's scarcity, blessings to the world's curses, newness to the world's decay, or joy to the world's sorrows."

"Earth has no sorrow that heaven cannot heal."

From Prologue 12

"Distressed feelings are underrated."

"Jesus loves humans, and when the humans you love become injured or threatened, the natural and godlike response is to get angry and feel the swell of energy directed toward righting a wrong."

"There is a reason why people say misery loves company. Sharing in one another's suffering binds us together in the deepest form of fellowship. It mysteriously draws us closer to the fellowship of Jesus' suffering as we, together, become like him in his death."

"Almost every book of the Bible was written by a sufferer."

"The psalms contain an abundance of lyrics that sound more like complaining, demandingness, dissatisfaction, anguish, anger, and protest than rejoicing . . . Do you think [God] would be hurt or offended if you start praying these words—*his words*—back to him?"

"Getting real . . . is unsettling, scary, even traumatic. Take the risk anyway and lean in."

"Sometimes the parts of the Bible we should pay attention to the most, and the parts of the psalms we should pray the most, are the parts that we have decided *not* to highlight or underline."

"Almost every person is insecure and underencouraged. Almost no person wants to admit it."

"Expressing distressed emotion in a broken world is a sign not of weak faith but of strong faith. It is a sign not of spiritual immaturity but of spiritual maturity. It is a sign not that we are unlike Christ but that we are like Christ. It is not a sign of weakness but a sign of strength."

"Laughter is God's gift to us. So are our tears."

"The call to rejoice in the Lord is not negated by our expressions of distress; it is honored and made complete by them. Our cries of anguish do not make us less human but make us more human."

"The fact that Jesus will come again is our reason to rejoice. The fact that he has not done so yet is our reason to lament, weep, wail, and hope. Though full and unmitigated rejoicing will come in the morning, now is also a time for tears."

"In every human heart, there is a God-shaped and God-sized hole. When we try to fill the hole with anything but God, the hole remains hungry and parched, because anything that is God shaped and God sized is bigger than the universe itself."

"Idols are tricky because they are usually good things. But in our foolishness, we turn them into things we cannot live without. But when we think that we can't live without something, in truth we are no longer able to live with it."

From Prologue 13

"People don't want to be pastored, taught, or led by a damaged person. Or do they? Maybe instead of labeling anxious and depressed people as damaged goods, we should learn from the psalms and Jesus and Paul about the biblical theology of weakness."

"God is upside down to our sensibilities. Better said, we are upside down to his."

"A healer who has not been afflicted is extremely limited in their ability to participate in the healing of others. But a healer who *has* been afflicted is strangely strengthened in their ability to heal."

"Many of the best therapists have themselves been in therapy. It's how God works."

"What feels like the scent of death to us may end up becoming the scent of life for others as we learn to comfort others in their affliction with the comfort that we, in our affliction, have received from God."

"Being afflicted does not make you ineffective. Being damaged does not mean that you are done."

"My afflictions may end up having greater impact than my preaching or my vision ever will."

"Our God is a tender God. He does not break bruised reeds . . . Our guilt and regret trigger his forgiveness, moral cleansing, and welcome. Our hurt and sorrow trigger his maternal tenderness and paternal protection. Our fear and doubt trigger his reassuring mercy and care."

"[God] has not called me to be awesome or to crush it at life or to be spoken well of and liked or to be a Christian celebrity or hero. These competencies belong to Jesus and Jesus alone."

From Prologue 14

"Once resurrected, our bodies will assume all the features of immortality, full redemption, unending momentum, untarnished flourishing, and imperishable bliss . . . Because Jesus lives and will never die again, the same must be true of us."

"Even the smallest amount of faith in Jesus is plenty. Why is this so? Because it is not the strength, nor the quality, nor the quantity of our faith that will get us Home. Rather, it is the strength, quality, and quantity of God's immeasurable goodness and grace and faithfulness that gets us Home."

"It is not our repentance that leads [God] to be kind toward us but his kindness that leads us to be repentant toward him."

"The breath you just took is one more toward your last . . . Life is wondrous and supremely difficult, and then we die. Nobody, even the author of life himself, gets to escape our last enemy, which is death. Until some of us do escape it."

"The current and coming chapters of our lives—including the ones that seem demoralizing or terminal—are but middle chapters in the Story of God."

"Death is not the end for us but is rather the final leg of our bent, busted-up, guilt-gutted, hurt-hindered, fear-wearied existence in a fallen world."

"Jesus Christ conquered and rejected death with a holy rejection. He hates death with a holy hatred. There is comfort to be had in this. On the other side of death, all of us who are in Christ will be able, once and for all and forever, to put erosive and life-sucking vandals like death, mourning, crying, and pain in the rearview."

"The most remarkable humans with the most remarkable faith are usually the ones who have come to the end of themselves, suffered deeply, and lost much."

"Beautiful people don't just happen. But when they do happen, even a wheelchair can become a pulpit, a chemo room a place of worship, chronic pain a path to holiness, burial dirt a plot of resurrection soil, and death a festival on the road to freedom."

From Prologue 15

"Our long-term worst-case scenario is *not* that we will rot in the ground. On the contrary, our long-term worst-case scenario is resurrection, everlasting life, and an ever-increasing, imperishable bliss."

"When Jesus says he is making all things new the Greek verb tense is unmistakable. He is saying that in the coming new heaven and new earth, he will make all things new *continually*. He will never stop making all things new. Every single minute, hour, day, week, month, year, decade, century, and millennium—forever and ever and ever—will be better and fuller, more life giving and satisfying, than all of what has come before."

"There is coming a day when we, his beloved children by faith, will feel younger, stronger, smarter, faster, happier, and more rested, tended to, and full hearted than we can even dream about currently. Our work will be fulfilling, even fun. Our play will be epic and unending. Our connection with God and each other will be a deep source of joy and fulfillment. Honesty will be effortless; deception, backbiting, and conflict will be impossible. Love will be the norm; hate, division, assuming the worst, echo chambers, and calling out to cancel will be distant memories."

"It is the object of our faith, not the size of it, that will get us Home."

"Dear sinning, suffering, Homesick friend, I pray God will give you confidence that your best days and years—your most golden, healthy, and happy adventures—are never behind and always ahead of you. In the new heaven and new earth, Jesus will continuously make all things new."

ABOUT THE
AUTHOR

S cott Sauls is husband to Patti, dad to Abby and Ellie, and senior pastor of Christ Presbyterian Church in Nashville, Tennessee. You can follow his author page on Facebook or connect on Twitter/Instagram at @scottsauls. He blogs weekly at scottsauls.com. His other books are also available wherever books are sold.